IMPROVE

EVERY

LESSON
PLAN

WITH

SEL

ASCD MEMBER BOOK

Many ASCD members received this book
as a member benefit upon its initial release.

Learn more at **www.ascd.org/memberbooks**

ALSO BY
JEFFREY BENSON

*Hanging In: Strategies for Teaching the Students
Who Challenge Us Most*

*10 Steps to Managing Change in Schools:
How do we take initiatives from goals to actions?*
(ASCD Arias)

IMPROVE
EVERY
LESSON
PLAN
WITH
SEL

Jeffrey **Benson**

ASCD

Alexandria, Virginia USA

1703 N. Beauregard St. • Alexandria, VA 22311-1714 USA
Phone: 800-933-2723 or 703-578-9600 • Fax: 703-575-5400
Website: www.ascd.org • E-mail: member@ascd.org
Author guidelines: www.ascd.org/write

Ranjit Sidhu, *CEO & Executive Director;* Penny Reinart, *Chief Impact Officer;* Stefani Roth, *Publisher;* Genny Ostertag, *Director, Content Acquisitions;* Allison Scott, *Acquisitions Editor;* Julie Houtz, *Director, Book Editing & Production;* Miriam Calderone, *Editor;* Thomas Lytle, *Creative Director;* Donald Ely, *Art Director;* Masie Chong, *Graphic Designer;* Valerie Younkin, *Senior Production Designer;* Kelly Marshall, *Manager, Project Management;* Shajuan Martin, *E-Publishing Specialist*

All web links in this book are correct as of the publication date below but may have become inactive or otherwise modified since that time. If you notice a deactivated or changed link, please e-mail books@ascd.org with the words "Link Update" in the subject line. In your message, please specify the web link, the book title, and the page number on which the link appears.

PAPERBACK ISBN: 978-1-4166-3001-2   ASCD product #121057

PDF E-BOOK ISBN: 978-1-4166-3003-6; see Books in Print for other formats.

Quantity discounts are available: e-mail programteam@ascd.org or call 800-933-2723, ext. 5773, or 703-575-5773. For desk copies, go to www.ascd.org/deskcopy.

ASCD Member Book No. FY21-6 (Apr. 2021 PSI+). ASCD Member Books mail to Premium (P), Select (S), and Institutional Plus (I+) members on this schedule: Jan, PSI+; Feb, P; Apr, PSI+; May, P; Jul, PSI+; Aug, P; Sep, PSI+; Nov, PSI+; Dec, P. For current details on membership, see www.ascd.org/membership.

Library of Congress Cataloging-in-Publication Data
Names: Benson, Jeffrey, author.
Title: Improve every lesson plan with SEL / Jeffrey Benson.
Description: Alexandria, Virginia USA : ASCD, [2021] | Includes bibliographical
    references and index.
Identifiers: LCCN 2020057232 (print) | LCCN 2020057233 (ebook) | ISBN
    9781416630012 (paperback) | ISBN 9781416630036 (adobe pdf)
Subjects: LCSH: Affective education. | Social skills—Study and teaching. | Emotional
    intelligence. | Social learning. | Reflective learning.
Classification: LCC LB1072 .B54 2021 (print) | LCC LB1072 (ebook) | DDC
    370.15/34—dc23
LC record available at https://lccn.loc.gov/2020057232
LC ebook record available at https://lccn.loc.gov/2020057233

30 29 28 27 26 25 24 23 22 21   1 2 3 4 5 6 7 8 9 10 11 12

*This book is dedicated to the memory and work
of Jim Grant of Peterborough, New Hampshire.
You called forth our better angels.*

IMPROVE
EVERY
LESSON PLAN
WITH
SEL

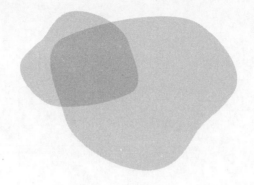

Acknowledgments

Special thanks to master teacher and my dear friend Lewis Gitelman. Your determination that I take this book the extra step—to directly confront the inadequacies of the status quo and reach for what we know is best for students and society—gave me the edge I needed.

Special thanks, too, to Lily Kofke for your incisive feedback; the moment was golden, sitting next to you with *your* hands on the keyboard making the changes.

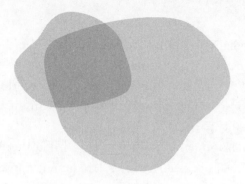

Introduction

For the majority of my career as a teacher and school leader, I have worked with students who were neglected, abused, exploited, and traumatized. They had learning disabilities and were emotionally fragile. They were marginalized, victims of institutional racism and homophobia, and excluded because they didn't fit the typical mold. They could find the daily expectations of school to be both soothing and anxiety provoking, depending on the day.

Their circumstances meant that my own experience of work each day was unpredictable, more extreme than what most teachers deal with on a regular basis. Students are not compliant robots in the machine of education; my students could never let me forget that. My article "100 Repetitions" (Benson, 2012) and my ASCD book *Hanging In* (Benson, 2014) were attempts to make sense of the chaotic, narrow, and deep niche within which I worked.

In those early years of special education regulations and the nascent research on best practices, I learned to teach my challenging (and lovable and courageous) students through trial and error. I leaned heavily into routines and rituals. In my little classroom at the end of the hallway in the basement, as far from the mainstream as we could be placed, I was told that what I most needed to do was keep my crew from disturbing the rest of the building. There was little expectation for me to have a robust curriculum, or belief in my students' capacity to learn it.

The upside of our isolation was that I had the freedom to do almost anything. I broke many rules, tried many approaches, shared much joy and frustration with my students—and more or less kept them safely out of everyone else's way. The downside was that no one knew or seemed to care what I was figuring out. In the faculty lounge during lunch, the other teachers would say, "We don't know how you do it down there all day, Jeffrey." I would nod, smile wanly, and think, "But I'm a teacher. I do what you do: I have lesson plans that I try to implement as best I can."

Developing lesson plans was my ritual of self-preservation. If I was going to be successful hour to hour, I had to engage, challenge, and support my bunch of outcasts from the mainstream in the essential commerce of schools: learning together. I sat down every day during my prep period and, like many teachers, at home on evenings and weekends, fearful that poor planning would lead to despair or disruption—probably both at the same time. I also had the hope, and some growing confidence, that with a lesson plan sewed up tightly, my students and I would experience the wonderful balm of success, despite all the forces trying to pull us into failure. Success is a healthy addiction, and lesson plans were my habit.

Confronting the Lesson Plan "Devil"

And then there was "the devil" (not in any religious sense, but rather as a Halloween-costumed character, a comical metaphor for my inner critic). As I would put the finishing touches on the next day's lesson plans, I would imagine "the devil" sitting across from me.

He'd grin maliciously and say, "Are you willing to bet me that your plan is going to work? Will it work for *every* student?" Those questions would stop me in my tracks. I'd feel a chill through my body and a knot in my belly. Why wasn't I willing to bet on my lesson plan?

Oh, right. I knew why. My student M. needed a graphic organizer for his essay, or he would sit staring silently, chewing his lip until it bled; V. had been out last week when we were learning one of the prerequisites and had a short fuse when she felt stupid; W. was likely to complete this task faster than the rest of the crew and could distract all of us when unmoored from a required activity. I clearly wasn't done planning; "the devil" would win this bet, meaning my day would be rough. I couldn't get up from my chair until I ran every part of the lesson plan through the filter of every student (which is why special education classes have to be so small). I had to get that graphic organizer ready for M.; I could sit V. with a friend who was good at sharing; W. would have a challenging extension ready to go. I would win that bet. I *had* to win that bet, for all of us.

I did have a few theoretical concepts to lean on. One big concept was constructivism (Brooks & Brooks, 2000), which I will reduce here to the simple notion that "telling is not teaching." I could not take what I knew and transfer that complex web of understanding directly into another human's brain in all the ways I understood it; teachers are not brain surgeons, connecting a few neurons in the grey matter of an anaesthetized patient. We need our students to pay attention, be involved, ask questions, try out ideas, and share their mental journeys; my students' fears, anger, past failures, and distrust made it hard for them to take those risks—the risks of trying. Even when they tried, they might reject their own well-constructed idea because they had constructed it themselves. My lesson plans, in my little education niche, needed to max out my students' capacity to try through every part of the lesson—or "the devil" would win.

Becoming Mainstreamed

So how did I get out of my little niche in the basement and become mainstreamed? Truth is, for the past 30 years, the world of education had been coming step by step toward me. There was a growing realization of the social, personal, and educational costs of isolating students with atypical learning needs, from students who were perpetually distracted in a crowded classroom to those who struggled to remember the sequence of multistep directions. The imperative for inclusion became the initial step into the mainstream—although for many students with atypical needs, the least restrictive environment may still be a classroom with only a handful of peers (but certainly not in the basement!). Inclusion demanded a degree of differentiation of lessons and curricula, buoyed by the increasing understanding of multiple intelligences. We always knew there was more to our students than failure.

The imperative for inclusion brought an increased focus on coteaching, grouping, and stations. The research on growth mindset (Dweck, 2006) was another step, giving us a common language for supporting a student's competence as a learner. We sadly saw how early in their tender lives some of our struggling students locked into the belief that they were not the "smart" ones and suffered for years under that crippling "fixed mindset" belief.

Most of my students were sure their exclusion from the mainstream was explained by their lack of intelligence. We now also know that intelligence tests are deeply flawed and culturally biased and predict very little about the long-term happiness of any person (Jensen, 2009; Ritchie, 2015). Literally no child has to be left behind. (Too bad that wonderful phrase devolved into an industry of testing.) We also know that solid executive functioning skills may be more critical for success, especially for middle and high school students, than any academic fund of knowledge (Cox, 2007).

Another step into the mainstream was the dissemination of publications about grit and resilience (Hoerr, 2017; Poliner & Benson, 2017). Imperfect as the concepts may be, perspectives on those two attributes strongly influenced the need to look at all the factors that contribute to academic performance. Educators who work with our most economically disadvantaged students always saw the grit and resilience those kids needed in order to overcome the barriers in their way (Love, 2019).

In retrospect, it is not surprising that the majority of my students came disproportionately from the least economically secure families in our communities. They were also disproportionately children of color. Wasn't it always obvious that students have a huge advantage if their lexicon, points of reference, customs, priorities, ways of building relationships, and belief systems match those of their teachers, the textbook publishers, and standardized test writers, most of whom are white?

The last few years have seen another stride forward: the long-overdue focus on racism, equity, and restorative justice, concepts that would have been welcome in my little basement community. The economic injustice that creates haves and have-nots remains a persistent impediment, battled daily by the enormous goodwill and ethics of teachers. I'll have more to say on this topic later in this introduction and throughout the book.

Many schools now compile scores for their student body on adverse childhood experiences (ACEs), including physical abuse, emotional abuse, domestic violence, household mental illness, and a number of other sources of trauma. We are discovering vast numbers of students whose fight-flight-freeze behavior in the face of school expectations is not a measure of their morality or motivation, but a well-learned response to the hardships they have faced. The notion of a trauma-informed school is no longer limited to out-of-district special education programs. Students with a history of trauma are everywhere. We have Response to Intervention (RTI), an approach that formalizes what innumerable special educators had been considering for decades. ASCD, among other organizations, has championed the whole-child perspective; indeed, the whole child walks into the school every day.

The acronym SEL (social and emotional learning) is now so common that I questioned whether putting it into the title of this book would attract or repel teachers. The Collaborative for Academic, Social, and Emotional Learning (CASEL) has become an internationally recognized resource. I am regularly asked to help schools develop a more SEL-informed culture, including improved adult-student relationships, a more inclusive set of activities to open the school year, nonpunitive discipline policies, and personalized learning. Principals want to know how their schools can be safe and welcoming environments for every child. I speak to school staff about how to hang in with their most challenging students, because we see that doing so is now everyone's job. I joke—truly joke—that I never knew how one could segregate students' thinking from their feelings—not in rituals, procedures, or lesson plans. All the above research now makes that assertion obvious and provides a pathway for expanding all students' likelihood of success in school.

I have been mainstreamed!

Embracing the Neuroscience— Without Adding to Teachers' Workload

Another development that is supporting the step-by-step progress of the past decades is the extraordinary research and applications of neuroscience. As noted, I knew I couldn't force my understanding into the brains of students; the best I could do was provide a safe place for learning, offer academic stimulation worthy of their attention, let them mess about (we will return to the seminal concept of "messing about" in Chapter 5), and then ask in some fashion, "So what's going on in your brain now?"

Neuroscience research affirms such a constructivist approach: the brain is endlessly plastic, growing interwoven networks of neurons, inspired by its own wonderful ideas. (Many thanks to Eleanor Duckworth [1996] for articulating that "the having of wonderful ideas" is a most worthy goal of all curricula.) My students' ideas might parallel mine but could never be exactly the same as mine or those of any other student.

SEL is also clearly supported by neuroscience, which confirms that our emotions and intellect operate in partnership; what our senses take in must pass through our emotional filters before entering long-term cognitive storage. In the absence of safety, our students' brains have more important survival business to do than figure out how to divide a fraction by a fraction. I assume most of us knew that all along.

But—and this is a huge *but*—all of these incredible possibilities for students' social, emotional, and cognitive development are being jammed into the already full agenda most teachers face every day. It is as if we are telling workers on a car assembly line to make the cars with fewer defects as we simultaneously speed up the assembly line, without changing almost anything about the structure of the assembly line itself. We demand more and more of teachers but not of the system within which they work. Despite the challenges, I have seen that most teachers implicitly recognize their students as social and emotional beings. Most teachers care.

This is not a book about "the revolution" to immediately upend the educational status quo (see me sometime to talk about that), and it is not intended to impose SEL as another curriculum. Anything but! What still remains at the heart of the entire school process, in the midst of all the expectations and chaos, are teachers with lesson plans, joining with a group of students. This is a book dedicated to lesson planning.

This book will help you synthesize all of the wonderful possibilities of a whole-child approach—social, emotional, and cognitive —into what you already have to do: make lesson plans. We'll see how a lesson plan that is intentionally and explicitly informed by SEL improves participation, builds trust, and sustains effort. We'll go back to the question "the devil" posed to me every night: "Do you really think that lesson can work for all the students?" And the goal is to reply, "You bet!"

Looking Beyond Lesson Plans

I hope this book conveys much more than a mechanical improvement to the daily grind of putting together and presenting a lesson plan. I intentionally want to convey a joyful, ethical, and soulful image of this extraordinary work we do in schools.

If you are new to the profession, I want to support your idealism and give you tools to hold that idealism with theory and determination. My stories are not just illustrations of strategies in action, but affirmations that we really can have great relationships with students, be innovative, and do the job well.

For veteran teachers, I want to provide a touchstone to counter the cynicism that can grow like mold in schools that have always lacked the resources we've truly needed. I want to counter the public skepticism of our efforts and the politicians who seem to know nothing about our work. I hope my stories remind you of your stories and all the profound prior learning you have accumulated day by day by day. The focus on SEL can reconnect you to what you love about working with students; most likely, your best moments of teaching have always been informed by the social and emotional learning of your students.

Writing About Institutional Racism and Inequity

Schools in the United States have been more successful institutions for children who come from families with white skin, economic stability, quality health care, and political clout. Every element of our schools conveys in its DNA the elements of the society from which it was birthed. There are many reasons for universal mandatory schooling, but whatever strands of history you pull together to weave the story of American education, the structures and outcomes are replicating the inequities born of our history of racism.

As I explored the possibilities for integrating SEL into each section of a lesson, I kept bumping into the ways that the institutionalization of racism and inequity permeate every one of those sections. Each part of a lesson contributes to the whole machinery of the school day and reveals the foundation of inequity. As a writer, I struggled with how often to point out, "There it is again!" I had no intention of simply finding one place in the book to check off the box of "Acknowledged Racism," as if nothing more needed to be said. But I did make decisions for where and when delving into the issue would make for a coherent reading experience.

As you read through the book, you'll see that for every "There it is again!" moment, I offer an explanation for how unacknowledged and unrepaired racism and inequity influence who is more likely to be successful because of their privilege, and who will struggle. I include suggestions and alternative pedagogical approaches in those moments. There are also times with students of any age when it is best practice to call out the systemic racism in our midst.

As a white man in my 60s, I continue to confront how racism has infected me; I am increasingly aware of the limitations of my perspectives. I hope to less often make statements that assume everyone has grown up constructing the same conclusions about our society and our schools as I have.

But I assume I have still fallen into unexamined habits of mind in this book. There are probably many moments when readers will wish I had seen once more the hidden power of racism in lesson plans and written, "There it is again!" I ask your forgiveness ahead of time. Exploring antiracist work is integral to any definition we have of SEL. Black lives matter in lesson planning; it is about time white people acknowledged that the lives of all students whose families have been structurally and relentlessly exploited and neglected matter everywhere.

How This Book Is Organized

The best lessons in life, the ones that have shaped our very character, do not fit into a predetermined lesson plan that has to be constrained to 38 minutes or 60 minutes or whatever your school's schedule demands. Granted, no one thinks the institutionalization of education into assembly line chunks is ideal. As one of my mentors told me, school schedules are a collection of innumerable compromises.

The chapters in the book follow a sequence of steps, or sections, in a traditional lesson plan. (An appendix provides a chapter-by-chapter guide for lesson planning related to SEL goals. This guide is also available for download at www.ascd.org/ASCD/pdf/books/BensonLessonPlanning.pdf.) I think all lesson plans should include every section, but that is likely not possible and only worth striving for within whatever time frame you must fit your lessons. The sequence of steps is as follows:

- The teacher starts with goal planning. (Chapter 1)
- The teacher engages students in learning as they enter the room. (Chapter 2)
- The teacher sparks students' interest and motivation by reviewing what they have been making sense of in recent lessons. (Chapter 3)

- The teacher gets students working with the specific objectives of the lesson. (Chapter 4)
- Students actively use and expand their skills as they explore the lesson's objectives. (Chapter 5)
- Formative assessment allows the teacher, with the full participation of students, to gauge their progress and identify next steps. (Chapter 6)
- An intentional closure routine solidifies understanding, scaffolds the completion of homework, and predicts a successful transition to the next responsibility. (Chapter 7)

Along the way, I will share ideas and tools for classroom routines that surround the lessons, but the heart of this book is the nitty-gritty of lesson planning and implementation. At the end of each chapter I offer answers to questions and include problem-solving tips, because a problem-free school day that addresses the whole child is a rarity. There are great days in schools, but rarely perfect ones.

You don't have to be perfect; there is no perfect. Do what you can, start where you are (let's assume you already have some SEL tools in your kit), and gain more expertise. We are all learners.

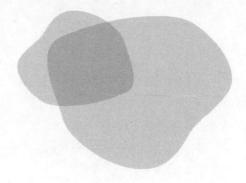

A Note About
Remote Learning

I wrote this book in 2020, during the COVID-19 pandemic—a time when many teachers have had to become adept at writing lesson plans for remote learning. In this book, I occasionally offer recommendations for adapting specific activities to this new reality. I trust teachers who take this book to heart and head will find many of their own ways to use the available technology to improve their remote learning plans with SEL. Technology will change, and the apps we use today may soon become antiquated, but all of the imperatives and joys of integrating SEL will remain, no matter what the setting.

1

Making SEL Goals Explicit

I was a suspicious student. From my earliest years in elementary school, I wondered why I was being told to do a lesson. I occasionally asked the teacher why we had to learn something, but after innumerable responses that seemed designed to tamp down my curiosity in favor of moving along, I stopped asking. I did the work to avoid getting in trouble. Every now and then, I found myself enthusiastically engaged, with no more understanding of what triggered that engagement than my distant ancestors had about the appearance of an eclipse: the moment happened and then it passed.

I can only wonder how much more I would have mastered, and how much more I might have contributed to the class, had I been given the opportunity to understand the teacher's goals, and to articulate goals of my own. The adults in school always operated behind an impenetrable wall of authority. I wish my teachers had known that "[a]dopting and strengthening a set of beliefs about mastery can become part of a learner's internal nature" (Frey, Fisher, & Smith, 2019, p. 77). Instead, quiet cooperation with the status quo was enough to get us through the day. My own ideas and those of my peers were deemed worthy only when they fit into a predetermined set of expectations: the lesson plan.

When I became a teacher, like most new to the profession, I wanted my students to have wonderful ideas of their own, and I wanted them to cooperate. I came to realize that when I said, "I need all of you to cooperate," I really wanted them to obey me. That's not an irrational desire—I am no fan of presiding over chaos—but obeying is not cooperating, and cooperating without understanding rarely inspires wonderful ideas. My students would need to know the goals and the roles that they, the students, played in our collective success if I wanted more than passive compliance. I *did* want more than that; passive compliance was all that had been asked of me when I was a student, and I did not want to replicate that culture in my classroom.

I became an early adherent of posting the agenda and learning goals of a lesson—now a common practice in many schools, the goals often preceded by the abbreviation SWBAT (Students Will Be Able To). By sharing the lesson's SWBATs, I believed I was inviting my students into the inner workings of the classroom machinery. For many students (and for adults too, as I came to realize as a college instructor and a principal), sharing the agenda and goals for our time together is often comforting; participants can reference where we have been, where we are, and what is left to accomplish. Nothing is startling. For the same reasons, most schools let students know when a fire drill or statewide testing is scheduled. With the agenda and goals posted, I could alert the students to our progress and check off the steps we had traveled.

I would read the goals and agenda to the class with a mixture of solemnity, bravado, and enthusiasm: "Today, we will be learning how to add fractions!" Some students would nod their heads, some would smile, others began to pull out their math folders, and a few continued to stare out the window. I am sure the students appreciated my efforts to share my excitement, and they knew, as they had learned early on, their role in passive cooperation.

Then one year, when I was teaching high school, I had a memorable student I'll call B. Almost every day, after my declaration of the goals and agenda, he asked, "Why are we doing this?" My explanations about the beauty of semicolons quickly left him with glazed eyes; my minilecture on the cultural and historic relevance of Shakespeare did the same. He'd sink back into his chair, as disconnected from the commerce of schooling as he had been for years. I took his alienation to heart; he was a lot like I had been, only more worn down.

I talked to a mentor of mine about B., because his persistence in asking why and never being satisfied was turning my empathy for him into annoyance. Maybe he didn't really care why at all and was only enjoying his ability to frustrate an authority. B. was very skilled in that regard. My mentor suggested I ask B. which *why* he was asking me.

"Maybe he wants to know why this lesson follows yesterday's lesson," she said. "Maybe he wants to know why adults think kids his age have to learn that lesson *this* year. Maybe he wants to know why it is on the SATs. Maybe he wants to know when and why he may ever apply this lesson in his adult life. Maybe he wants to know why you want *him* to learn this lesson. Maybe he wants to know why you care so much. Ask him which version of *why* you should answer."

That's what I did. When B. asked why, I offered a list of responses I could give him (which meant I had to be prepared!). On many days, he did choose one of the options ("Yeah, why do *I* have to learn this?"), engaging me in a worthwhile dialogue that often gained the attention of everyone else, ultimately helping us all be more purposeful —the active version of cooperating. On many days, when I offered B. the opportunity to choose which *why* I should address, he would wave me off, as if his questioning that day was more out of habit than need.

What I learned from B. (our most challenging students are often *our* teachers, inspiring us to gain more tools out of necessity) is that I always held a number of learning objectives in each lesson—some of them part of the "implicit curriculum" (Milner, 2017). More important, I found that the time spent engaging students in *understanding* all the explicit and implicit SWBATs supported their autonomy, their persistence, and their mastery. The two minutes of conversation paid many dividends.

In the ensuing years, I have seen many school leaders mandate that SWBATs be posted for every lesson. Unfortunately, I have observed only a small handful of teachers who truly make good use of that practice. I don't see anything wrong in the practice, just not much right, and not much understanding. I've seen students be given the chance to read the SWBATs aloud for the class and, more rarely, at the end of the class, to nod yes or no as to whether they have finished the lesson. I've never seen posted, alongside the traditional SWBATs, the SEL goals almost all teachers implicitly hold for their students in every lesson. Teachers' compliance with posting SWBATs is eerily similar to students' compliance with reading the SWBATs and then doing the work. When actions by both children and adults are done merely out of compliance, we aren't motivating for mastery.

How SEL Skills Lead to Mastery

Making explicit and discussing the previously implicit SEL skills in your daily lesson, right from the start, takes you way beyond passive compliance, paving the way to engagement, ownership, and mastery. Engaging students of any age in understanding the SWBATs presents you with a daily opportunity to build their SEL skills, because cognitive and emotional engagement involves overlapping and interwoven brain activity; cognition and emotions happen cooperatively to create understanding in each of us (Immordino-Yang, 2016).

Yes, doing this requires an upfront investment of time. The first day you introduce the activity of understanding the daily SWBATs may take 5 to 10 minutes; once the routine is in place, the activity should take 1 to 2 minutes. There will be days you may skip this step completely because the work is so clearly an extension of the prior day's SWBATs or you are in the midst of a unit that requires only an occasional reflection on the SWBATs. The important notion is that your students will be doing more than nodding in passive compliance; they will be learning about themselves in the very act of understanding the goals of your lesson.

Identifying the SEL Skills You Promote

My colleague John D'Auria asks teachers, "At the end of the year, how would you like your students to be different as learners as a result of their work with you?" Everyone has an answer, and if those answers are distilled into their essential elements, they would resemble the SEL qualities that are the focus of this book. Those answers, the implicit curriculum, are often the reason two teachers can be handed the same required textbooks and work in classrooms of the same size and shape, with the same number of students who come from the same communities, and yet the experiences of the students in those two classes over the course of the year will be significantly different. The students will be randomly encouraged, supported, and given feedback day to day on varied SEL skills.

I am urging you to make explicit and intentional the ways you want your students to develop SEL skills. I am urging you to share your investment in those SEL skills in the same manner you may be sharing the traditional SWBATs.

More than sharing, I am urging you to *sell* your students on those intentions. Students' SEL skills are obviously important to us as teachers—and essential for our students to be productive members of our classes, the school, and the larger communities in which they will live. The act of intentionally reinforcing those skills improves the likelihood of your students learning them.

Doing so may be particularly important for secondary school teachers. Few middle and high school teachers would say, "My adolescent students are socially skilled and masters of their emotional lives." Even in the midst of our content-laden, required curriculum, we are inevitably helping our students develop their SEL skills, reminding them to use good manners and reprimanding them when their tone is disrespectful to us and others. More than SEL serving simply as a rubric for disciplining poor behavior, our work includes preparing students for far more than the final exam and the standardized tests. We should righteously complain that the size of our classes, the imposed requirements, the pacing guides, and the mandated textbooks undermine our ability to personally know every student, but few of us have given up on being more than machinelike conveyors of SWBATs.

Most secondary school teachers I know long for and cherish the social and emotional connections we can make with even a handful of students each year. This book is a guide to reclaiming our fully human commitments to ourselves and to our students: from kindergarten to 12th grade, we can explicitly teach the whole child.

Essential SEL Skills for All Ages

There are various lists of SEL skills that explicitly support students' development. Some lists are so extensive that many teachers would find them overwhelming; few people could remember all the skills, much less assume responsibility for teaching them. Other lists are more concise but contain abstract skills that require mastery of many specific subskills—for example, "delay gratification." How do you teach a student to do that?

For this book, I've synthesized the lists into a concise set of easily observable SEL skills (see Figure 1.1). These are skills that teachers reinforce through in-the-moment feedback, through occasional

FIGURE 1.1

Essential SEL Skills

Skills for Self

Emotional Self-Awareness
- Using words to identify feelings
- Identifying triggers
- Developing self-soothing strategies

Personal Goal Setting
- Making short- and long-term goals
- Developing plans to meet goals
- Analyzing progress and making adjustments

Identifying Strengths and Supports
- Identifying your strengths
- Advocating for needs and resources

Interpersonal Skills

How Others Feel
- Identifying emotions with verbal cues
- Recognizing nonverbal cues

Working with Similarities and Differences
- Identifying varied perspectives
- Communicating understanding of others' perspectives
- Developing solutions that account for varied needs

Communicating with Others
- Asking others how they feel and think
- Expressing your feelings directly and respectfully

Skills as a Community Member

Having an Impact on Your Community
- Matching your behavior to the setting
- Admitting mistakes, apologizing, making amends
- Assessing the impact of your actions on others

Socially Responsible Decision Making
- Recognizing the needs of others
- Predicting and evaluating outcomes of actions
- Using feedback to adjust behavior

Contributing to the Greater Good
- Identifying opportunities to make a positive impact
- Taking actions to promote positive changes

coaching sessions, and, most important, by modeling in everyday interactions. These are skills that most teachers already ask their students to demonstrate and randomly support throughout the year. These are skills that are understood by students of all ages but are demonstrated in different ways as children grow up. For example, 1st graders will use a much smaller vocabulary to tell us how they feel than a high school student will use, but we can certainly expect all students to demonstrate age-appropriate ways to talk about their feelings.

This book will support your efforts to intentionally develop those essential SEL skills as your daily lesson plans unfold. It's not a new curriculum; this is the curriculum that almost all adults work on with children they care for.

SWBATs and Racism

Sharing and discussing my agenda and SWBATs as a teacher was another way to account for my ignorance of the lives my students had lived before walking into my classroom. Many of my students of color and other exploited communities had never seen how the goals of schools fit their needs, except as a distant vision of something that, if they were very fortunate, might happen after high school gradua- tion. Better said, too many of my school's goals did not fit their needs; unfortunately, they were seeing the world of school and their world outside of school accurately (Fergus, Noguera, & Martin, 2014).

The lesson plans derived from such far-off goals present a daily motivational hurdle for too many students. Dropping out, as either a passive act of indifference or a physical act of turning away from the entrance to the school, is a process that unfolds over years of alien- ation. Bringing students into the conversation about SWBATs and the SEL skills that matter to them is a powerful and necessary ritual of inclusion. Schools and classrooms that declare their goals and explicitly manifest them in all their daily business can help our most disregarded and disenfranchised students share in what should be *our* collective mission (Fergus et al., 2014).

Regarding SEL skills and discipline, there is much evidence that students of color, particularly Black males, are disciplined more often than their peers for such actions as talking back to adults. One teacher may find a Black student's tone disrespectful and a trigger for disciplinary actions; another teacher may use the interaction as a teachable moment, helping the student match behaviors to the setting (one of the essential SEL skills); a third teacher may praise the student for taking the risk of self-advocacy in the face of authority and the historical institutional racism that permeates all of our institutions. Self-advocacy is another essential SEL skill.

What I have learned from many astute educators is not to label the student, or the student's actions, as categorically "disrespectful." The legacy of racism, built on the power of one group to enforce its cultural norms on another, remains as tinder for conflict between students of one culture and persons of another—often students of color and white teachers. Even with a student who looks like me, I cannot assume that I am an able representative of that student's parents or community.

I have learned to say, "Let's try this again" when spoken to in ways that I once labeled as disrespectful. I offer the student a rephrasing or suggestion that works for me—for example, "If you would lower your voice to about the volume I am speaking now, I would be happy to continue to talk with you." I am not making judgments about the student, but giving the student guidance about talking to *me* in that moment.

The authority of my position as an adult in the school gives me the right to make demands on young people, but "disrespect" remains a culturally laden label that we can avoid. Instead, I model for my students essential SEL skills: using words to identify my feelings, identifying my triggers, advocating for my needs, and expressing my feelings directly and respectfully.

Action Steps

Take a moment to answer these questions about *your* current SEL curriculum, referencing the Essential SEL Skills chart (Figure 1.1).

- Which skills do you consistently and explicitly reference with your students?
- Which skills do you implicitly reference, and with what wording?
- Which skills do you only occasionally reference, either implicitly or explicitly?
- Which skills do you rarely, if ever, reference in any fashion?
- Which skills would you like to make more explicit and intentional in your practice?

Your answers to these questions will give you your starting point for integrating SEL skills into lesson plans. You may have looked at the SEL skills list and said, "I work with students on that skill!" Now you can commit to working on that skill development more intentionally. You might be thinking, "I could be reinforcing another skill, especially with the group of students I have now." In both cases, this book will build your tool kit of intentional strategies for teaching the SEL skills that matter to you.

The Power of Praise

From my years of observing teachers, I have seen and heard them randomly praise students for exercising SEL skills. Most commonly, teachers will prompt students to say "please" and remind them to say "thank you," scaffolding students to practice "Skills as a Community Member." Few students are confused by the reminders to say please and thank you to adults.

Praise is an underused tool to reinforce SEL skills—underused when the intention to build specific SEL skills remains at the implicit level. But praise is powerful! Being recognized by a trusted adult for doing well triggers the release of brain chemicals that flood us with good feelings about ourselves, making us more likely to repeat the behavior that brought us praise. In terms of your SEL-related intentions for your students, praise is a powerful pedagogical tool.

Many educators have long urged teachers to praise students as many as five times for every reprimand they deliver. Praise helps you condition your students to use SEL skills, fostered by the good feelings your praise stimulates, until those skills become habits. Students from early elementary grades through high school are constructing their SEL skills as foundation blocks of their character, and your praise matters at every age.

Praise obviously should vary according to the age of your students. Here's how praising a student who is "advocating for needs and resources" might sound in different grades:

- **Grades K–3:** "I like so much how you asked for another color crayon! Please keep asking for the things you need."
- **Grades 4–7:** "Absolutely get yourself another marker! Keep asking for what you need to get your work done well."
- **Grades 8–12:** "I like that sound of self-advocacy. Go get what you need."

Rehearse saying aloud the SEL skill-building prompt you would be most comfortable saying to your students. I assure you that with just a little practice, you will easily find your own comfort level for explicitly praising your students when they demonstrate an SEL skill. Throughout this book, you will find many models of SEL skill-building prompts to use in the classroom; the opportunities are abundant every time you are with your students.

> **Action Steps**
>
> Referencing the Essential SEL Skills chart (Figure 1.1), answer the following questions:
>
> - Which skills do you explicitly praise students for using?
> - Which skills can you praise more often to meet your SEL expectations for your students?

How SEL Skills Are Implicit in Lessons

Learning in school is a social activity. The traditional skills of being polite are perhaps the most obvious tools for working with others. However, SEL skills that contribute to academic success are present in *every* lesson plan. Consider the following examples:

- The lesson involves a review of basic skills previously taught; students will need to identify their strengths to know where to put more effort into learning.
- The lesson will take place over a period of days; students will need to analyze their progress and make adjustments.
- The lesson has many challenges in it, and you expect and want students to work at the outer edge of their capabilities; students will need to use self-soothing strategies to manage their frustration.
- The lesson requires students to work in small groups; they will need to understand how others think and feel and how to express their own thoughts and feelings clearly and directly.
- The students are choosing a project for a social justice fair; they will need to predict how their choices will promote positive changes in the school.

Action Step

Examine one of your lesson plans. Referencing the Essential SEL Skills chart (Figure 1.1), identify the SEL skills your students will need to engage in the lesson's activities in order to maximize their learning.

SEL Skills and the SWBATs

Earlier I questioned the ritual of sharing the daily SWBATs with students. The main reason I did so is the significant lack of student engagement that the ritual commonly evokes. I have not seen students being expected to make sense of the SWBATs, or to see how the lesson fits into their own journeys as learners, or to anticipate the effort required of them to reach proficiency or mastery. For most students, the events of the class move along as if the SWBATs had never been shared.

But consider the potential benefits of students making sense of the SWBATs, of connecting those learning targets with their own needs, and of anticipating the effort they will need to put forth to be successful. That's a lot of benefits! The one to two minutes students spend thinking about and sharing their reactions to the SWBATs will help them find a personal commitment to engagement, give them access to their strengths, and reduce the amount of repetition and reteaching that is often the result of student uncertainty and anxiety as a lesson is launched.

SEL skills are essential tools for managing the cognitive tasks we give students in every lesson. Including those SEL skills in the standard SWBATs makes explicit and open for consideration what the human brain does silently in every moment: manage the feelings that accompany all sensory input.

Once you have identified the explicit SEL skills you want the students to practice in a lesson, as you did in the preceding Action

Step, you can share those skills along with the standard curriculum SWBATs. You may write the SEL skills on the board next to the SWBATs or simply talk about them. Share your enthusiasm for this aspect of the lesson; after all, the only reason to explicitly share the SEL goals is because they matter to you! *The SEL skills do not require a separate set of activities to promote student mastery*. Once you have made those SEL skills explicit, the opportunities to practice them begin as soon as the students know the SWBATs.

Turn-and-Talks for SWBATs

The research (McTighe & Willis, 2019) is robust on what happens in the human brain when we get confirmation that we are correct in our judgments: our brain releases chemicals that can build focus and persistence. To leverage that biological boost and set students up for success, have them engage in a brief turn-and-talk with a peer, sharing their answers to these three questions:

- What am I going to be learning?
- What strategies will help me learn?
- How will I be asked to show my learning?

The one or two minutes devoted to this activity will save countless more minutes of checking in with students who are struggling to know what to do. The brain research is also clear on what happens when we are anxious and uncertain: we can go into fight-flight-freeze mode, which does not contribute to rich learning. Conversely, a state of calm anticipation maximizes our focus and memory. The SEL development in a turn-and-talk itself is robust as well, and it supports many of the skills you want your students to develop as they navigate the traditional academic curriculum.

Steps for a Turn-and-Talk

The turn-and-talk comprises three steps:

1. Students are presented with the goals, expectations, and directions. This step addresses the fact that we are feeling creatures; new information and sensations must pass through the parts of our brains that manage emotions before being processed by our higher-order thinking. I remember how I felt at the end of the first day of each semester in college, having been given the syllabi and what seemed an impossible-to-complete mountain of work required of me in every course. I was sure I would fail something. I would have to talk myself out of dropping out (flight mode). I reminded myself of my previous academic achievements and remembered that there would be no college graduates if it were literally impossible to do this work.

I have been with students of every age who, upon hearing the expectations of a lesson, unit, test, or course, are flooded with doubt that they will be successful. I have learned that we can't expect students to have confidence without a measure of acknowledged competence. Far too many students don't have the confidence to raise their hand and say aloud in front of all their peers, "I am confused" or "I am worried I will fail." Sitting in silence, they experience degrees of cognitive shutdown. They may retreat into a fixed mindset (the opposite of a growth mindset) and say to themselves, "I am not really smart enough to do this." Letting them know that they will all have a moment in their turn-and-talk, in private with a peer, to get organized and ready to work will benefit all students—and be essential for many. Some students may have simply been confused by the directions, and the support of a peer builds their mutual SEL skills and moves the lesson along.

2. Students are given think time to prepare their contribution to the turn-and-talk. We should provide think time for every expectation and question we present to students. The fact that a small handful of students raise their hands right away does not mean they are smarter than their peers, nor that the rest of the class has nothing to say. Too often, the pace of school reinforces the false notions that speed is intelligence and quickness is wisdom. Think time is essential for including all brains in the commerce of the class.

I give students 30 seconds of think time before a turn-and-talk because I don't want them to ramble. I want them to decide how much and what they want to share, prompting the SEL skills of using words to describe their feelings, identifying their strengths, and advocating for the supports they will need. You may find some of your students need scaffolding to use think time well—for example, "Make a speech to tell your peer what...."

3. Students reflect on answers to the three questions about today's SWBATs. We all spend a large part of our lives talking and listening to another person. In the one to two minutes of their turn-and-talk, students not only get clarity about the cognitive expectations of the lesson but also are deeply engaged in exercising SEL interpersonal skills. Depending on the age of your students, you can scaffold them all with a prompt, differentiating the SEL skills for this class and for particular members of this class. Here are some examples:

- "What words let you know how confident your partner is about today's work?"
- "In what ways are you feeling the same about the work as your partner, and in what ways are you feeling different?"
- "Is there a question you want to ask your partner to be sure you understand what they feel and what they need, so you can help them make their work plan?"

Teacher Prompts

Teacher prompts for a turn-and-talk will vary, depending on grade level. In each of the following examples, students are working in pairs, and the SWBAT is "Students will be able to prepare for tomorrow's quiz"; the teachers make the SEL skills explicit and intentional, blending those skills with the academic task:

- **Grades K–3:** "Children, when you are talking with your neighbor about the quiz, I'd like to hear each of you ask your neighbor if they are a little nervous about the quiz or not nervous at all. If someone is a little nervous, I'd like you to help them make a plan to be calm. Think of all the ways we have learned to be calm this year! You will be working on two skills that are *so* important and that we have been practicing all year: asking how your neighbor feels and making plans together."

- **Grades 4–7:** "Class, I know not everyone is happy about taking a quiz. When you get into pairs to review the SWBATs, the first thing I want you to do is ask your partner how they feel about the quiz, how ready they are, because people need different types of support if they are feeling nervous or confident. We've been working on these two skills a lot this year—asking how people feel and making plans. This is a time to look at our vocabulary list of words that communicate feelings and use a few more abstract words in your dialogue. Don't assume you know what your partner thinks and feels. Find out! Then make a study plan."

- **Grades 8–12:** "Everyone, I know there are a lot of things you'd rather be doing than studying for this quiz. So when we pair up to review the SWBATs, the first thing you should do is ask each other about your motivation for studying. Is your partner as motivated as you are? Is your partner ambivalent? Don't guess—ask questions to find out. Once you've established how much each of you cares about studying, make a plan to help each other. We've been doing this all year: not assuming you know what someone else feels, but respectfully asking questions to find out more and then choosing strategies that fit each person. Be yourself, and help each other."

Making Your Own Goals Explicit

A few years ago, I was hired to lead a professional development workshop for a school district on the first day faculty were back from their summer break. I was excited and honored to be part of this annual renewal of our profession. In the hallways and offices, I heard colleagues greeting one another. I saw teachers in their class-rooms hanging up posters. The air was buzzing with purpose and anticipation.

The faculty headed to the auditorium for the annual welcome from the superintendent. He gave a brief hello, acknowledged the newly hired faculty, and then launched into a presentation about the revised teacher evaluations, the updated attendance software, and the changes in billing procedures for purchases. The excitement in the room whooshed out like the air from a balloon pricked with a pin. The faculty trudged from the auditorium after an hour.

The superintendent missed the moment—a moment to remind us all of our deeper purpose for being in the building that day and to leave us inspired. Of course, he needed to communicate the business end of his responsibilities, but not at the cost of deflating our collec-tive excitement about being with one another. The only mention of our collective and individual goals was lost in the bureaucratic minu-tiae contained on one page of the revised teacher evaluation form.

Goals should not be reduced to a line item on a form—not for teachers, not for students, not even for administrators. I once worked with a principal who fully embraced and shared her own goals. She led by example as her school committed to explicitly fos-tering growth mindsets—not just for students, but for everyone. She would begin each staff meeting telling a story of an error she had committed that week, what she had done to amend for her error, and what she was learning from that process.

Imagine for a moment if that superintendent who plunged into business had instead first shared his own goals for growth, and had given an example or two of ways he was committed to sticking with the goals through the school year. I believe the collective commitment of the faculty would have been elevated.

Actions of those in authority carry great weight; sharing goals gives explicit permission for everyone to be evolving as learners. Roland Barth, a wonderful principal and mentor, had a sign over the door to his office: Head Learner. When teachers share their goals, they are building a learning *community*, which is much more than a room where everyone simply gets through the curriculum. As is the case throughout the book, the theme of moving from the implicit to the explicit and intentional will provide a path into SEL—in this instance, the academic and SEL learning that comes from sharing goals.

Most teachers work extremely hard; if their only goals were to fulfill all of their responsibilities, that might be enough. But I also know most teachers want to do more than get through the year. They often have implicit goals that are based in social and emotional domains: enjoying the students, enjoying their colleagues, getting along with the administrators, effectively partnering with parents, and taking care of themselves.

Before we consider SEL goals for students—and appreciate the ups and downs of their journeys—take a moment to appreciate your own intentions, your own SEL goals. Just as in the case of the principal who got on stage to share her growth-mindset goal and commitments, when teachers share their learning goals with students, the entire class benefits. I once worked with an art teacher who was taking a course at a local college to improve her watercolor skills. When she spoke to her own students about the joys and struggles she experienced in learning watercolor techniques, every student got a lesson in lifelong learning. Emotions are contagious, and modeling how to learn is great pedagogy. The art teacher's students respected her more than ever as a result of her sharing her goals.

I think of my student B., who wanted to know why *I* cared about my lessons, about him, about the world. When I shared my goals, he might not have been enthused to do the lesson, but he could feel the power of someone whose goals drove his actions and commitments.

Action Steps

Referencing the Essential SEL Skills chart (Figure 1.1), consider the following questions:

- Which skill(s) would you like to focus on for your own professional fulfillment?
- How might you share that information with your students? (Not all goals have to be shared with students; there are times when privacy must take priority.)
- In what ways do you think your students would react to your sharing your goals with them?

SEL Goals and Academic Achievement

Given that we are social creatures and that school is such a social setting, most students have implicit SEL goals. The point of teachers sharing their own goals is to normalize making SEL goals an explicit part of their dialogue with students. In fact, even though high school classes are typically those most wedded to a traditional content-driven curriculum, high school students are the *most* developmentally prepared to make their SEL goals explicit, and the most capable of assessing how their SEL efforts are affecting their academic achievements. With students of any age, identifying SEL goals is not a separate curriculum; in fact, as noted earlier, the SEL curriculum is happening every day in every class. I strongly suggest that investing a few minutes at the start of each year to make everyone's SEL goals explicit will provide immeasurable benefits for relationships, classroom management, and academic achievement.

Steps for Supporting Academic Success Through SEL Goals

You can support students' academic success through SEL goals by using a four-step process. The first three steps take less than five minutes to complete; the fourth step blends easily into all the actions described in this chapter that support students working with the standard academic SWBATs. Here are the steps:

1. Review with students, in age-appropriate vocabulary, the Essential SEL Skills chart (Figure 1.1).
2. Share (if this does not violate your privacy needs) your own SEL goal(s).
3. Encourage students to pick their own goal and share it with you. For the youngest students, take notes as students share. For older students, have them take a minute to write their goal in a note to you. One reason for you to share aloud your own goal is to normalize this part of learning.
4. When students are answering questions about the daily SWBATs, periodically ask them to note how practicing their personal SEL goal will enhance their efforts, something you can do at any transition during a lesson. The act of bringing to mind the SEL goal makes it more likely that students will discover the moments in the lesson when applying their skills can support their efforts.

Teacher Prompts

Here is how reminding students to apply their SEL goals in the lesson can sound at different grade levels:

- **Grades K–3:** "Before we head out to recess, think for a moment about your SEL goal. I am thinking of mine, which is making sure I use words to let you know how I am feeling. I want to be ready to say to someone who is not being careful, 'I am scared you are going to get hurt. Can you please move more carefully?' Think now about how your SEL goal can make recess fun and safe. During recess, I will be asking you how you are using your SEL goal."

- **Grades 4–7:** "We started the new unit yesterday, and looking at your exit tickets, I can see that many of you are nervous about doing well. As you know, my SEL goal is to use your feedback to know how much support you need. I have some ideas. Before I share those, take a moment and think about how your SEL goal can help you to manage this unit. For instance, a bunch of you had goals regarding making plans. Some of you had goals for advocating for support. Those seem in line with where we are now. Whatever your goal is, take the next 30 seconds to consider how that goal can help you manage this unit. Today's exit ticket will ask you about your SEL goal."

- **Grades 8–12:** "You are going to be in small groups today, providing critiques of each other's work. This is a great time to make a commitment to use your SEL goals. You all know I am working on relaxing while you are in small groups, giving you the responsibility of asking me for support when you need it. I will do my best to trust that you will ask for what you need. The first thing I want you to do when you get in groups is to go around and share what your own SEL goals are and how applying them to group work can improve everyone's outcomes. When we get out of the small groups, the first question I will ask the group's reporter is to what extent you appreciated the time to share those SEL goals."

Questions and Answers

What if a student cannot or does not want to pick or share an SEL goal?

First, make sure you have shared your own SEL goal with the class. Assure the student that it is OK to not pick or share at that time.

Let the student know you will ask again another time. You might ask the student if there is an SEL goal on the Essential SEL Skills chart that is already a strength, and tell the student the goal can be to keep up the good work. Even if the student does not acknowledge the goal, you can continue to praise the student.

Is merely referencing the Essential SEL Skills chart and talking about it enough to teach the actual SEL skills?

Doing so would be a big start. Every day, students are randomly exhibiting age-appropriate SEL skills. By highlighting those skills, praising the students' use of them in the moment, and anticipating how they can be applied to a lesson, you are stimulating students' brains to explicitly make efforts to use the skills. At times, you may have to provide brief directions—for example, "When you ask someone how they feel, keep good eye contact and wait quietly for them to answer." Most teachers do versions of such prompts already, but their prompts are disconnected from an ongoing effort to reach mastery. Going from the implicit to the explicit and intentional will help students develop the skills.

2

The Start of the Lesson: Gaining Students' Interest and Motivation

When I was a teacher, I wanted my classroom to be more attractive to my students than the hallway; when I was a principal, I wanted my school to be more attractive than the streets. I think a lot about the first moments students step into our academic spaces and how to reduce as much as possible their unproductive fears of failure, of shame, of being seen as just another kid sitting in a chair struggling to fulfill a demand, a kid whose feelings and beliefs and aspirations rarely seem to matter to the machinery of schooling.

I wanted my students' first experience to be one of engagement and success, because I wanted to demand more of them; I wanted them to demand more of themselves than passive compliance. A mentor of mine said, "Every element of the school day is part of the curriculum; kids are developing ideas about the world they live in and their role in that world all the time. Be conscious of all the moments when you can make a difference."

As students enter the classroom, the opportunity to make a difference will be enhanced when you make explicit and intentional your now implicit SEL curriculum. Before students get to their seats to find out the day's SWBATs or to begin the first activity awaiting them, they are learning.

> **Action Steps**
>
> Referencing the Essential SEL Skills chart in Chapter 1, ask yourself the following questions:
>
> - Which SEL skills do you implicitly promote for your students as they walk into the room?
> - Which of your routines, procedures, and expectations promote students' opportunities to exercise those skills?
> - What additional routines, procedures, and expectations could more intentionally and explicitly allow students to exercise the SEL skills that matter to you?

My observations suggest three common activities that promote SEL skills as students enter classrooms, before they dive into the first academic demand:

- Being greeted by the teacher
- Getting settled into their chairs and the surrounding space
- Engaging in jobs to help the classroom be organized

A closer look at each of those activities will suggest explicit ways you can encourage students to more effectively exercise the SEL skills that matter to you.

Teacher Greetings

I think every student, every day, should be personally acknowledged by a teacher. Some teachers stand by the door and say hello by name to each student, and, when appropriate, students can have the option of adding a handshake, a high five, a fist bump, or an elbow bump (and for early elementary students, a hug). Some teachers circulate through the room as students settle into their seats, making eye contact with each and giving a personalized message to a few ("Love your socks," "I'm glad you're feeling better; we missed you yesterday"). In remote learning settings, teachers can still say hello to each individual student. Acknowledging each student pays big benefits for subsequent engagement in learning. Students who feel acknowledged for who they are will be three times more likely to indicate that they push themselves to do better academically (Quaglia & Corso, 2014).

In the ritual of greeting, adults model caring and demonstrate to students the impact of SEL skills—positive feelings course through our nervous systems into every part of our bodies. With support and modeling by adults, students can also exercise the SEL skills of using words to identify their feelings as we greet them ("You look upset. Are you OK?") and give them a chance to ask for support ("Let me know if there is something you need for today's project"). We prime them for academic focus. In the following examples, teachers are reaching out briefly to one student in particular as the others settle in:

- **Grades K–3:** "Good morning, M. Can you tell me how you feel? I'm excited about today, and I really need you to put away your coat so I can start class. Is there anything I can do to help you now?"
- **Grades 4–7:** "Good morning, M. I'm super-ready for today's lesson. Are you super-ready, kind of ready, or not so ready? OK, thanks for letting me know. Is there anything I can do to help you be more ready?"
- **Grades 8–12:** "Good morning, M. I'm anxious to start class quickly because we have a lot of items on our agenda, and I know you want to get to your project. Tell me a word or two to

describe how ready you are for the work. OK, what I need from you is a lot of undivided attention for the first five minutes. What do you need so you can stay focused?"

Getting Settled

Teachers who greet students at the door are helping them transition from the hurly-burly environment of the playground, cafeteria, hallway, or street into the unique academic culture of the classroom. During the few seconds when students walk to their seats, they need to use SEL skills to further their transition to academics—their success at engaging those skills can be the difference between a successful or an unsuccessful lesson. Some students need to use the SEL skill of self-soothing, reminding themselves that they are in a safe place to take academic risks; others must apply the SEL skill of matching their behavior to the setting of a classroom; a few will benefit from the SEL skill of reconnecting to their goals. Here's how teacher prompts can engage students in exercising those SEL skills:

- **Grades K–3:** "Friends, as you walk to your seats, please give yourself a big hug to fill your body with good energy."
- **Grades 4–7:** "When you get to your seats, write at the top of the worksheet one strategy you will use to keep from being distracted during our quiet work time."
- **Grades 8–12:** "Everyone, the first Do-Now task as you walk to your seat is deciding the most important thing *you* want to focus on during this class, because that is what you will do best."

Classroom Jobs

Elementary students often have jobs that help the classroom operate efficiently: sharpening pencils, cleaning boards, straightening books on shelves, watering plants, feeding the fish. Many of these jobs happen at the beginning of the day, helping the students take ownership of the space, furthering the transition into the academic arena, and supporting many SEL skills related to communicating with others and contributing to the greater good.

It's odd, then, that our older students are asked to do so little to maintain the classrooms they use and thus further develop their SEL skills. When I taught in secondary schools, I always sought out volunteers for tasks that I could delegate, allowing me to focus on greeting students, prompting their SEL skills to be ready for academics, and providing me the precious time to give one or two students a little extra attention.

Among many jobs in my middle and high school classes, one of my favorites was the class DJ, a coveted job that rotated weekly. The class DJ chose a song each day that played while students came into the classroom. Other jobs for adolescents at the beginning of class include taking attendance, collecting and distributing materials, adjusting lighting, conducting surveys, and keeping track of time. Many adolescents want to contribute to the greater good, which is a developmentally powerful SEL skill set for teenagers. They are seeing the world with fresh eyes, with all of its possibilities and faults. Adults should intentionally allow them to make a difference in their daily school environment by offering them partnership in setting up the classroom culture.

Action Steps

Keeping in mind the SEL skill-building possibilities as students enter your classroom (greeting students, supporting their self-care as they settle in, engaging them in jobs that build the classroom community), consider the following questions:

- What opening-of-the-classroom activities do you already do?

- In what ways can you more intentionally support the SEL skills in those activities?
- What activities might you add to your repertoire at the opening of the classroom that engage specific SEL skills?

"Do-Now" Meets SEL Skills

I am a big believer in providing students with a "Do-Now" activity as the academic transition into the classroom. From a behavior management perspective, the Do-Now gives students a productive focus when they might otherwise succumb to socially mischievous impulses. If students are being mischievous, rather than merely telling them what to *stop* doing, I can show them what to *do*—a specific positive channeling of their energies.

The Do-Now is part of every day, another signal that this classroom has a culture different from the hallways. At its best, the Do-Now explicitly supports a wide range of SEL skills, including personal goal setting, identifying and leveraging one's strengths, and contributing to the greater good.

A successful Do-Now sets students up for the entire lesson. When students experience success, their brains release dopamine, a chemical that activates feelings of satisfaction. That initial feeling can enhance "attentive focus, motivation, curiosity, memory, persistence, and motivation" (McTighe & Willis, 2019, p. 10), which is exactly what we want from the Do-Now: a springboard into accepting the challenges in the coming lesson.

I have been in many schools where Do-Nows are mandated, the same way posting the daily SWBATs is mandated. And sadly, just as the ritual of posting and sharing the SWBATs can devolve into an activity without meaning (as discussed in Chapter 1), the Do-Now can also become meaningless, just another chore to check off. The rich possibilities for enhancing your SEL priorities through the Do-Now can succumb to the repetitive dullness of compliance.

The most problematic aspect of a mandated Do-Now is when it consists of only one task—from my observations, an all-too-common experience. A small number of students (ones I am sure every teacher can predict) will successfully engage with that one task; other students will struggle; some students will give it a shot and quickly discover their limitations. A few will opt not to try at all rather than confront their limitations yet again, and those students are then more at risk for mischievous behavior. For traditionally strong students, the one-task Do-Now reinforces their positive growth mindset. For too many others who have not yet experienced enough success to take risks, their fixed mindset will be reinforced; their failure to connect with this one task will evoke all the feelings of incompetence they carry with them into class every day.

Students who connect with and have the academic skills necessary to complete the single Do-Now activity will get that positive dopamine springboard effect. Unfortunately, many students will come into class, look at the single Do-Now expectation, and turn away—the springboard looking more like a high-dive platform requiring a long walk up a steep ladder rather than a pleasant dive into warm waters.

How common is it for students to be excited rather than fearful to start an academic task, to dive into the Do-Now? Almost one-third of students report they are scared to try and fail in school (Quaglia & Corso, 2014). No single teacher is likely responsible for that fear. Teachers are required to persistently test and grade students on curricula that are often most accessible for students from more privileged backgrounds; the system routinely undermines confidence as much as inspires it. For many students, the SEL skill of personal goal setting in school becomes one of emotional survival, a series of maneuvers for not getting caught being wrong (Jacobson, 2013).

The first academic task of the day must explicitly counter the expectations of failure that millions of students experience as they walk into school. A Do-Now *with choices* is one of my favorite ways of telling every student from the moment they settle into their seats, "Your brain and thoughts belong in this room."

Do-Nows, SEL, and Equity

A sense of belonging is critical to learning. Neuroscientist (and former high school science teacher) Mary Helen Immordino-Yang taught in a diverse middle school with many students living in poverty. When she taught her classes the evolutionary biology that explains skin color, their usual indifference to the curriculum was upended, their questions revealing a deep need to understand the lesson in personal and emotional ways. She writes, "It is literally neurologically impossible to build memories, engage complex thoughts, or make meaningful decisions without emotions" (Immordino-Yang, 2016, p. 18). Her students' cognitive passions were ignited by the lesson on skin color, and she kept that passion burning by her willingness to engage their curiosity. Their whole selves belonged in her class.

A Do-Now with choices can ignite students every day, making the classroom a place that belongs to them. More specifically, we don't have to shy away from acknowledging the issues of racism and inequity that for decades have affected the lives of so many students. It's not a hush-hush secret. They know, and schools must acknowledge the reality of students' lives. When teachers of any color and level of privilege invite the world of their students into the lesson, the curriculum can become "our" curriculum. We all belong.

Belonging engenders a feeling of safety; in the absence of safety, we experience stress, and stress interferes with learning on cognitive tasks (Jensen, 2009). Alfred Tatum (2005) puts it bluntly for

Black male students: they feel like "captives in a hostile environment" (p. 39). Students who have been victims of systemic poverty and racism and who have far too infrequently seen themselves, their needs, and the aspirations of their families in the curricula, are most at risk of disengaging from another undifferentiated task, such as a one-size-fits-all, mandated Do-Now. The singular Do-Now is not a way to create a broad and safe academic environment.

But a differentiated Do-Now, with options that engage a variety of learning preferences and interests, is a big part of a classroom culture that can "signal to the brain a sense of physical, psychological, and social safety so that learning is possible" (Hammond, 2015, p. 45). Upending a school experience that engenders fear in one-third of students by transforming your classroom into a welcoming environment—from how you greet students to their very first academic challenge each day (the Do-Now)—is essential SEL work. That essential work includes leveraging every opportunity to integrate SEL skills into what you are already doing in class.

Do-Nows and the SEL Skills of Contributing to the Greater Good

Earlier I mentioned three SEL skills in particular that can be the focus of a multichoice, differentiated Do-Now: personal goal setting, identifying and leveraging one's strengths, and contributing to the greater good. Rarely do standard curricula identify "contributing to the greater good" as an outcome of the lesson, but explicitly and intentionally slipping such a prompt into the Do-Now provides more motivation for engagement with the day's lesson.

Helping young people contribute to the greater good by working toward transforming the world into a more equitable and safe environment is not likely what many think of in terms of SEL skills—but the *"social"* element of SEL is not limited to being polite. It includes understanding the emotional cost of inequity and oppression (for early elementary students, of "being treated meanly") and seeing oneself as an advocate for change in one's community. Those are not typical SWBATs and will likely not be the basis of questions on standardized testing. But a Do-Now that places the curriculum in the ever-evolving world of your students boldly sends that strong message at the start of class: "Your brain and thoughts belong in this room."

Here are Do-Now prompts that can apply to almost every lesson and can sound very similar at all grade levels:

- **Grades K–3:** "How would people be able to get along better if everyone learned what we learned yesterday?"
- **Grades 4–7:** "Imagine everyone in your neighborhood learned yesterday's lesson. How might that help the neighborhood be a better place?"
- **Grades 8–12:** "If every person on Earth learned yesterday's lesson, in what ways might the world function better?"

Action Steps

Based on a recent lesson you taught, consider the following questions:

- How would the world be a better place if everyone learned that lesson?
- How do you think your students would answer the above question?

Do-Now Options

For many teachers I have worked with, allowing their students—of any age and ability level—to freely choose their Do-Now activity from a menu of options is a leap of faith. Most fear that students will choose the easiest task, avoid a challenge, finish quickly, and then be susceptible to mischief as they wait for their peers to finish their work, but this has *almost never happened* in my decades of providing multiple Do-Now options.

My experience is that the novelty of having choice and control, and experimenting with that responsibility each day, is a chance to avoid boredom. Making wise choices to take care of one's needs is an SEL skill that can last a lifetime. Quite the opposite of creating behavior management issues, my multichoice Do-Nows reduced off-task behavior.

Overwhelmingly, my students chose the Do-Now task that was intriguing to them—a manifestation of working at their growing edges, in the appropriate spaces in their zones of proximal development. In the words of Souers and Hall (2016), "If we limit children's ability to experiment and explore, how will they develop self-concept and self-confidence?" (p. 160). Perhaps the leap of faith is remembering that human brains are inherently curious when not constricted by fear.

When I began offering multiple Do-Nows, I was inspired by thinking of particular students who were often disengaged—for example, "What option will E. find interesting?" Then I thought about giving my traditionally strong students challenges worthy of their confidence in themselves. As I came to realize how much meaning and classroom management could be garnered from offering a menu of Do-Now activities, I considered options worthy of every student: each of them deserved a chance to see themselves in that first academic demand of the day.

I began to look forward to preparing the Do-Nows. One might say I was engaging my own SEL skill development: identifying my needs, my goals, my sense of contributing in this small way to a more equitable world. With just a little practice, I developed the ability to create multiple Do-Nows quickly, as have many teachers I have mentored.

From this practice, the following six Do-Now options emerged that activate SEL skills, as students make choices based on their emotional needs, their academic goals, their strengths, and their evolving sense of purpose in the world:

1. Repeat an essential skill from the previous few lessons with no changes. Long-term memory is not a stable process in the brain but one that requires periodic review to maintain accuracy and ease of retrieval (Medina, 2009). Many students know they need more repetition to secure their understanding. These students will benefit from repeating the exact same task they have seen before. They will also exercise the SEL skill of taking care of their learning needs by choosing this option.

In Chapter 3, "Accessing Prior Learning," we will look in more depth at various ways to prompt students to recall and expand their understanding of recent lessons. This Do-Now prompt is certainly part of accessing prior learning, as are several of the following options.

2. Repeat a task from the previous lesson with minor changes. Many students have no need to do the exact same task, and if that were the only Do-Now option, the lack of emotional engagement would diminish any deep learning. But the chance to be successful by applying the work from previous lessons to a similar task will satisfy their need to grow.

3. Extend the task from the last class into new territory. Offer students of any age a chance to climb up Bloom's taxonomy (discussed in Chapter 6) by doing one of the following:

- Pair up a student who was absent the previous class with a peer who will teach the basics of the lesson (combining the skills of analysis with many SEL interpersonal skills).
- Ask how the skills from the previous lesson can help the student in a scenario you provide.

- Allow students to list all the ways they and others can use the skills of the previous lesson to make the world a better place. (I have rarely been more pleased and surprised by my students' answers than when reviewing their response to this option, a clue that they long to engage the SEL skill of contributing to the greater good.)

4. Show the skills in a completely new way. Offer the option to draw a picture, make a structure, design a graph, write a rhyme, or even dance in a way that translates and applies the previous lesson, allowing students to develop the SEL skills of identifying their strengths and contributing to the learning of others (a form of contributing to the greater good).

5. Foreshadow the coming lesson. Ask students what they think about an idea that will be part of the day's lesson, which can be shared as a list, in prose, or in dialogue with a peer. Encourage them to think of stories from their own lives that might apply to the coming lesson.

6. Ask, "What are you thinking most about today?" This option never changed in my daily Do-Nows. There are usually a couple of kids who initially have too much on their minds to engage successfully in an academic task; they need another form of transition into the classroom. The SEL skills of using words to communicate feelings, developing self-soothing strategies, and advocating for needs represent a worthy set of goals that matches the academically rich opportunities of the other Do-Now options. This option allowed me to expect some form of engagement from every student.

Action Steps

Referencing the list of six Do-Now options, consider the following questions:

- Which of those six Do-Now options do you generally choose?

- Which SEL skills are implicitly exercised through your typical Do-Nows?
- Considering the lesson you identified in Chapter 1 (or another lesson you are planning), what Do-Now options can you offer your students going into that lesson?
- Given your current group of students or particularly challenging students in your classes, which SEL skills might you want to explicitly prompt them to exercise through expanding the Do-Now options? Design a Do-Now option for those students in the coming lesson.

Metacognition, Do-Nows, and SEL

The human mind is bombarded by stimulation in every waking moment, from input through our five senses to the endless stream of thoughts and memories we continually generate. Sifting through all that stimulation requires us to actually forget a lot if we want to remember the important stuff. Our brains look for patterns and want to create a coherent story of what just happened—or as we teachers put it so simply, to learn (Medina, 2009).

I was fascinated by the decisions students made in picking their Do-Now activity. When my planning allowed me to ask a few to share their decision making, I learned how they were managing their own learning. In telling me, they too came to understand more about themselves as active learners because, as Duckworth (1996) notes, in the simple act of "trying to understand a child's understanding, the child's understanding increases in the very process" (p. 96).

Metacognition is the understanding of what just happened in our brains. Unfortunately, students are often required to transition from one activity to the next with almost no time devoted to constructing a coherent story of what just happened. Our standardized curriculum of having students memorize academic content and skills is not the same as allowing them to reflect on their process of learning in order to build a coherent story of themselves as learners.

Giving students a few moments to reflect on their effort, goals, planning, and execution of plans will enhance their SEL skill development. Even brief reflection will provide enormous growth, because "the more attention the brain pays to a given stimulus, the more elaborately the information will be encoded—and retained" (Medina, 2009, p. 74). The daily Do-Now is an excellent tool for metacognitive reflection.

You can scaffold students' retention of their experiences of themselves as learners, and build their SEL skills in the process, through a few prompts. If you can't envision having the time to add a metacognitive reflection every day after the Do-Now, schedule such time only once a week. Perhaps Monday will be the "metacognitive day" in your class. Monday is particularly good for such activities, as a simple reference to Monday's metacognition on Tuesday or Wednesday will activate the part of the brain still retaining Monday's metacognition. Prompts also signal to students the importance of their SEL skills—again, without having to teach a separate SEL curriculum. Prompts help them sift through all the stimulation of the Do-Now (or any activity, as we shall see throughout this book) and pay attention to its SEL components.

Depending on the age of the students, the following metacognitive prompts can be followed by silent reflection, a quick turn-and-talk, writing in their SEL journals, a few students sharing aloud to the class, or inclusion in homework:

- "Did you choose a Do-Now today that was a real challenge, or something that seemed fun and creative, or did you need a calming task?"
- "Did you feel better, worse, or the same after you completed your Do-Now?"
- "Which of your strengths helped you finish your Do-Now?"
- "If you fixed an error in your Do-Now, what did you learn from making that fix?"

- "Given what happened today with the Do-Now, do you have any goals to work on in tomorrow's Do-Now?"

Questions and Answers

How can I find the time to give feedback and grade all these Do-Nows?

You don't have to grade everything students do! Some days, you may require students to pass in their Do-Nows, not for grading as much as for assessing their efforts and understanding. You might have time to circulate through the room as students work, greeting them and taking a little longer at particular students' desks to note their efforts. If the schedule of the day allowed me the time, I would ask some students to share their Do-Now work aloud. I have also often asked students to voluntarily pass in their Do-Nows if they would like me to look at their work, saying, "I'd especially like to see your Do-Now if you are happy with it and think I will be happy looking at it, or if you want me to know what was hard for you."

In an educational culture that has become driven by high-stakes testing, giving students the freedom to pass in a Do-Now because they want you to know what they delight in, or what is hard for them, once again sends the message that all students belong in your room. The Do-Now is the transition into the academic and intellectual culture of your classroom. Let's keep that doorway wide open.

What about the students who need the threat of being graded to take the Do-Now seriously?

Many teachers I have worked with are concerned about the small number of students who will continue to avoid work and accountability if the Do-Now is not being graded. This concern feeds into a standard practice in most schools: we deny the vast majority of students the freedom to make choices (a huge SEL skill builder!), for fear that a few will abuse that freedom of choice. We have to turn that paradigm on its head. We *will* allow the vast number of able students their autonomy, while scaffolding the few others to do better. Consider that we don't say, "A few of you students are clearly not ready to learn algebra, so no one will be learning algebra"!

For those few students who avoid work, you can discreetly ask them to pass in their work or spend a little extra time with them during the Do-Now. Here's a good challenge: design a Do-Now option that is specifically targeted for the interests and strengths of your most noncompliant students!

How do I help my academically weakest students have a successful Do-Now experience?

First, there is no need to ever say, "Option 1 is easy. Option 3 is really hard." As I mentioned earlier, I never found that my academically strongest students gravitated to a Do-Now that was easy for them. And there are students for whom "easy" option 1 might be the perfect level of challenge. Let them make that choice without your judgment, as they build the SEL skills of working from their strengths and analyzing their progress on goals.

I did worry that my students with learning disabilities would start on a task that might quickly overwhelm them and reinforce a sense of incompetence. I don't need to completely shield them from making an error in their choices—all students have a right and a need to occasionally stumble as they learn to work at the edges of their abilities—but some students will be better served by having a successful academic experience than stumbling again. That's a judgment call. For those students, I would give them an enthusiastic greeting and steer them to a good option, saying, for example, "Would you please try option 4 today in the Do-Now? After I wrote it up, I thought about you because that task requires drawing lines, and you are great at drawing lines! I want to know if I was right when I guessed you would like that task."

Doesn't the Do-Now take more time away from the required curriculum?

The Do-Now is usually dependent on the required curriculum and provides students a personalized opportunity to delve deeper into the skills and content of the curriculum. If you are already a Do-Now practitioner, providing multiple options doesn't change the amount of time a given student spends on a task.

3

Accessing Prior Learning

A funny thing happened on my way to writing this chapter: I kept avoiding the task. Despite my prior experiences publishing articles and books, my tool kit of writing strategies, the success I felt from the two chapters of the book already saved on my computer, and a contractual deadline to complete this manuscript, I continued to find other tasks around the house to engage my time.

I was feeling a sensation of near nausea when I imagined opening the file to plunge into this chapter. Many students have told me of their similar physiological fight-flight-freeze reactions as they faced the blank page when assigned to write an essay, or stepped into a math class, or thought about participating in team sports in gym classes. What was going on with me?

I looked at the list of SEL skills from the prior chapters. OK, I needed to honestly identify my feelings and what was triggering them. I had to figure out the resources I could use to get through this episode of avoidance. I had to remember that pushing through the avoidance was part of my commitment to contributing to the greater good.

I chose a first step: to review the outline for this chapter; and that's when I realized that I was worried about not having enough to say on the subject of accessing prior learning. My outline was paltry; no wonder I was worried. Perhaps I had reached the limit of my competence... and then what? Each moment of feeling worried and incompetent increased my experience of being worried and incompetent, like the image of a snake eating its own tail. Feeling worried and incompetent to meet the challenges of this task was not a motivator! And it isn't for students, either.

I assume many of you have experienced such moments. Under stress, the human brain narrows the scope of its focus to safely get through the moment; the future (for me, how great I'll feel seeing my new book published) is not as powerful a pull as the present felt experience (Eagleman, 2015). Avoiding the feelings that the current challenge is presenting has its rewards—in this case, escaping the feeling of incompetence—however temporary that escape may be.

Luckily, a friend had just sent me an article about accessing prior learning. Like someone jumping into a life raft floating by a sinking ship, I jumped into reading the article and saved myself from drowning in the depths of my felt incompetence—and avoided for a little longer looking again at the blank opening page of this chapter.

The article was good, but its impact was sensational. Almost as soon as I finished reading the initial paragraphs, I felt my mind light up. I quickly clicked open my meager outline and started jotting down ideas. One idea led to another, and those ideas led me to remember a story about a student that reinforced a notion about prior learning that connected to all sorts of SEL concepts. I pulled a book from my shelf—there was a quote somewhere in it that could nail the transition I'd need later in the chapter. I was soon reminded of other quotes, and then recalled experiences of helping students to access prior learning, experiences that had accumulated from all the years of working in schools but had been blocked from my thinking by my barrier of worry.

My revival illustrates the impact of accessing prior learning and why it is a critical part of the daily lesson plan. Students construct new learning on the foundation of what they already have learned—and crucially, what they can retrieve in the moment from all the activities, memories, and lessons accumulated from their lives in and out of school. The brain literally destroys many fragile memories every day to prioritize what must be remembered, and in a typical school day, we try to cram countless names, dates, processes, and concepts into our students. All that input is too much for most students without systematic and periodic review. Information that is not reviewed within three or four days may never become stable and integrated with other long-term memories (Medina, 2009).

Accessing prior learning stimulates interwoven neural networks of facts, understandings, interests, and emotions. As teachers, we are always in competition for the attention of our students' brains because the brain prioritizes its energy expenditure on a "need to know" basis (Eagleman, 2015). The Do-Nows discussed in Chapter 2 *spark* mental activity; accessing prior learning *focuses* that activity.

When students are feeling the pleasure of remembering prior learning, they are neurologically more ready for the next lesson. Cognitive pleasure, physiologically enhanced by the release of dopamine, provides fuel for attention and persistence. That fuel also provides energy to reconnect with their SEL skills of committing to long-term goals, working with their strengths, and contributing to the greater good.

Being ready for the next lesson—having access to prior learning —requires the whole child to be engaged. Not surprisingly, we remember most the experiences that connect to our emotions and needs. Compliance is no match for really wanting to understand more, based on what the brain already understands and needs to know in order to be satisfied. In Chapter 1, we looked at ways the SEL goals we hold for students—and they hold for themselves—can prime them for academics. The same is true for the lesson at the juncture of accessing prior learning.

Including All Students

Accessing prior learning invites all students to belong in the class, because their brains hold memories and summaries of events in the idiosyncratic ways they have come to know the world. Those ways of knowing are shaped by culture, by privilege, and by one's place in the long road of history. Zaretta Hammond (2015) notes that our physical brains are the hardware we use to learn, but our culture is the software through which all stimulation is processed and understood.

This point is critical for teaching in a multiethnic and multiracial country. The connections I have made to the curriculum as a white, Jewish, urban, heterosexual, American-born man—the idiosyncratic ways I make sense of and access knowledge—can be vastly different from the cultural bedrock of my students. My access to prior learning of times tables as a 3rd grader was embedded by setting up folding chairs in rows for a community meeting. The physics of suspension bridges I studied in middle school was wedded to my familiarity with the cables and towers of the Brooklyn Bridge near my home. Students who have not grown up as members of the dominant culture, with its pervasive resources, references, and assumptions, still have their own resources, references, and assumptions. As we will see later in this chapter, casting a wide net to access prior learning will grab hold of the diversity of connections that make up the collective understanding of all of our students. They all have the need and the right to be primed for the coming lesson. Their culturally embedded references, goals, hopes, and connection to community and the greater good—the stuff of SEL that readies them for academic success—are readied by accessing *their* prior learning.

A Big Pitfall

In Chapter 2, we looked at the risks and limitations of providing a single Do-Now activity. Providing only one access point for any classroom expectation will exclude students. Unfortunately, there is a widespread, substandard, one-size-fits-all routine in schools for attempting to access prior learning, and it sounds like this: "Class, who can tell what we did in yesterday's lesson?"

Inevitably, a small number of the same students each day take the risk of guessing what the teacher wants to hear. A few of those students—the ones with fast language-processing skills or a set of references that they assume the teacher shares with them—will have their hands up before the teacher finishes the question. Often the teacher calls on one of those students. *Perhaps* the rest of the class listens to the answer.

At other times, teachers will cold-call on a student to guess what the teacher wants recalled from previous lessons ("A., what do you think the answer is? We haven't heard from you in a while"), or the teacher picks a name randomly from a collection of Popsicle sticks inscribed with students' names. Students who are not confident that they know what the teacher wants to hear—often a large number of the students—hope they won't get called on. The experience of being singled out among peers to publicly display a lack of learning—the inability to guess what the teacher is thinking—is a daily stressor for literally millions of students.

Meanwhile, the students who are confident that they can guess what the teacher is thinking are waving their hands, anxious to be called on and recognized for their memory skills and for their ability to talk in public. Perhaps they want to rescue their less confident peers from embarrassment—a wonderful SEL skill (involving socially responsible decision making, knowing how others feel) that even our youngest elementary students exhibit.

All that social and cognitive activity happens during the minute the class plays the game of "Guess What the Teacher Is Thinking," but what does *not* happen in that minute is a rich accessing of *everyone's* prior learning—all those interesting and idiosyncratic connections and fragments of understanding in every student's brain. For many students, the "Who can tell me…?" opening prompt is just another minute to get through unscathed.

We should never forget that the brain's first task is survival, and that primal goal can hijack the rest of the brain's capacity. When students are not anxious about surviving the moment unscathed, they have the mental capacity for remembering their personal goals and strengths, considering how they will contribute to the greater good, and leveraging those SEL skills to dive into the depths of their memory to retrieve something worth sharing from previous lessons.

The Best Prompt for Accessing Prior Learning

Here is a simple and powerful alternative to "Class, who can tell what we did in yesterday's lesson?" This prompt sounds exactly the same from kindergarten to 12th grade: "Class, let's all think quietly for 10 seconds. Your job is to remember anything you can from what we have recently been studying. There are no wrong answers. The only right answer is anything you can recall."

Every student's brain is invited to participate. There is no expectation to guess what the teacher is thinking. No single student does all the cognitive work for the class because that is impossible, of course. And, an important point, no single student can provide all the answers to all that happened in class.

In addition to the benefit of involving just about every student in searching internally for prior learning, I love this minute of class because I get to hear their funny and wise answers. I get to hear the full range of their diverse thinking, all the culturally and person-ally crafted understandings that make us a community. As the class listens to all the responses, our brains light up with appreciations and the innumerable connections woven through our vast neural network of memories and concepts. The SEL skills of sharing one's perspective, listening to and appreciating other perspectives, and contributing to the greater good are deeply reinforced in this simple daily activity.

I have heard the following responses, among so many, after asking the class to search their personal memories for a morsel of learning to share from the prior class:

- "I remember when T. figured out what A. was explaining."
- "I remember that it's a good idea to check my work twice before thinking I am done."
- "I remember the formula for the area of a polygon."
- "My mother told me a story about when she was learning English and had to study what we did."
- "I remember when the pigeon landed on the windowsill."
- "I remember when you wrote *15* on the board when the answer was *51*."

My students were always willing to remind me of errors I had made, and those responses typically sparked connections to what we were doing when I made that error. Some students took pleasure in making us all laugh and groan by repeating exactly what they had shared the day before, but I didn't mind; the repetition helped us cognitively, and the laughter and groans made our class a safer place to be ourselves. Every one of their answers brought us all back to prior classes and initiated cognitive access to those lessons.

Often, their responses clued me in to the level of understanding they carried from one day to the next. I could then cherry-pick from their responses the key ideas I wanted to reinforce or reteach. For a quick assessment of their collective understanding, after a student's contribution, I could ask the other students to signal if they agreed with the accuracy of that contribution or had something to add at that time.

I didn't want to fool myself into thinking I had everyone's attention for a reteach by ordering everyone to pay attention, because, really, we can't make that happen by dictatorial fiat. I first gained their attention by the prompt ("What do *you* remember?") that activated their infinitely unique and wonderful memories. Each contribution to our collective memory triggered the neural wash of dopamine in their brains. Then my affirmation and the affirmation of their peers further enhanced their capacity to pay more attention for the coming lesson.

Another Opportunity to Make SEL Skill Building Explicit and Intentional

Because of our brain's need for repetition and review of learning every few days, I suggest articulating at least once a week how sharing memories of prior lessons can explicitly and intentionally develop students' SEL skills. This is how that prompt might sound for different grade levels:

- **Grades K–3:** "Class, when you share what you remember, you will help everyone remember! I also know that you will hear things from your friends that will make you realize how smart everyone is in their own ways. And by listening to your friends, you will get better at listening!"
- **Grades 4–7:** "Class, it's time to put our ideas and memories together for all of us to grow. This is a time when each of you helps everyone to learn. You will have to practice active listening to learn from one another; I know some of you have an SEL goal to be better listeners. I think all of you are totally

interesting people, and no two people remember exactly the same things from the last lesson."

- **Grades 8–12:** "Class, it's time for our collective brain, the brain of this class community, to grow. Anyone who has the SEL goal of contributing to the greater good—and a lot of you do have that goal—will improve that skill when you share. And the more we listen to and learn from one another, the smarter we get. That's the benefit of listening to people who have ideas you don't have. I know many of you have a goal of being more sensitive to the diversity in the world, so by respectfully listening to the diverse memories here in class, we honor diversity."

Action Steps

Ask yourself the following questions:

- Imagine asking your next group of students what they each remember from recent lessons. What do you think you will hear?
- Given the personalities and needs of your group of students, which SEL skills would benefit from being explicitly practiced as you access all their prior learning?

There is a saying from the world of therapy: "There are many ladders into the pool"—that is, many ways to get a human brain to probe its depths. The pool of prior learning is accessible through ideas, memories, and feelings, and we want to get students to wade into those cognitive waters. The article my friend sent to me on accessing prior learning got me wading into the many areas of my brain that I needed to access in order to write this chapter. Before urging our students into the deeper waters of the next lesson, our task as teachers is to first get them swimming confidently in that direction.

Activities for Accessing Prior Learning

The list of suggested activities presented here is not exhaustive. I hope that the ideas trigger your commitment to this step in the lesson, reminding you of what is already in your tool kit and adding to your options.

I have included activities that students can do solo, in pairs, in small groups, and as a whole class. In each activity, I list the SEL skills that are most often engaged by the activity, but there are usually other SEL skills that students can practice, boosted by how you introduce the activity. *What you explicitly articulate in your instructions will prompt an increased attention to those particular SEL skills.*

Choose activities that work best for all of your interests in any given lesson. In every activity in the list—as in every time you create a safe space for students to share more than "guess what the teacher is thinking"—you give your students the opportunity to practice the SEL skill of contributing to the greater good. Here are my suggestions:

1. Display an image that you displayed before or an image that is similar to one from previous lessons. Ask students to share their memories and ideas triggered by that image.
   SEL skill: Appreciating similarities and differences
2. Ask students to list ways the SWBATs from prior lessons connect to the essential question of the unit.
   SEL skill: Connecting learning to personal goals
3. Set up stations visited by small groups, with each station asking students to share their answers to one of the following prompts:
   • What activities did we do last class?
   • What do you remember thinking about in that class?
   • What vocabulary words got used a lot or were new?
   • What was a funny or interesting moment in class?

SEL skills: Asking others what they think and feel; recognizing the limits of one's own perspective

4. Class bingo: Distribute cards with a question in each box based on recent lessons—words, moments, facts, vocabulary. Students walk around the room, finding a peer who will share their understandings and help them fill in that bingo square.

   SEL skills: Identifying one's strengths; identifying resources

5. Display for the class a specific fact or process from prior lessons. Ask students to share what else they know, what they now want to know more about, and any tangential ideas and stories that come to mind based on that fact or process.

   SEL skills: Analyzing progress; matching behavior to the setting (in what students choose to share)

6. Display the unique, frequently cited, or new words that have been part of recent lessons. Ask students the following:

   • In what ways are they remembering what those words mean?

   • How might people use those words outside school?

   • How do those words support people communicating their thoughts and feelings?

   SEL skills: Using words to identify feelings; identifying strengths; appreciating varied perspectives

---

Action Steps

• Considering recent lessons, what were the SWBATs your students most likely need to have reinforced before the next lesson in the unit?

• Based on the list of suggested activities, develop in your lesson plan activities that will help students to access and reinforce those recent SWBATs.

• Identify the SEL skills that you generally prioritize for this class. How will you prompt students to pay attention to those skills in this accessing prior learning activity?

Questions and Answers

Do I have to do the step of accessing prior learning as part of every lesson?

Other than greeting every student, I am not sure there is any one thing you absolutely have to do in every lesson. What we know from brain science is that new information and skills link up with prior learning to be remembered; the new stuff first finds a home within the old stuff. I have heard it said that the opposite of "to remember" is not "to forget" but "to dis-member"—that is, what we wanted to recall never found *member*ship in established networks of the brain, and so it floated away. The time you spend on accessing prior learning can be a 30-second silent recall of recent lessons or one of the longer activities listed above. I strongly recommend frequently reviewing all prior lessons; otherwise, the never-ceasing delivery of lessons day after day that is the basis of prescribed curricula is truly overwhelming for too many students.

Isn't the Do-Now activity you advocated for in Chapter 2 a lot like accessing prior learning? Can't I combine them into one activity?

Yes, I am glad you noticed that! You can absolutely craft Do-Now prompts that engage prior learning; many of mine do. Here's the biggest way they are different: the Do-Nows serve as a reentry not only into the cognitive business of the class but also into our routines, and so they can have a wider range of options than prompts that are restricted to accessing prior learning. An example is "Tell me what is most on your mind walking into class." That said, I think you can develop a large enough repertoire of prompts to effectively make the Do-Now and accessing prior learning a single activity to start every lesson.

In Chapter 2, you argued not to worry about grading the students' responses to the Do-Now prompts. Is the same true for accessing prior learning?

Yes, yes, yes! Accessing prior learning is not a quiz. Students are so accustomed to trying to guess what the teacher is thinking—what the right answer is—that if this step is graded, they will quickly see accessing prior learning as another time when their own memories, ideas, and connections are ignored by the machinery of the school. All the richness of their wonderful and idiosyncratic neural brain activity will be collapsed into avoiding wrong answers. That's the opposite of the cognitive and emotional conditions that promote readiness for the lesson ahead.

4

Providing and Receiving Direct Instruction

First, here's a synthesis of this entire chapter: students can learn a huge portion of the curriculum without direct instruction. Our brains evolved to learn from the stimulation of our senses, taking in the experiences of the environment and finding patterns. In Chapter 5, we will consider student exploration and experimentation as an equally valid path of constructing understanding. You can skip this chapter if you find direct instruction anathema to your educational philosophy.

That said, allocating time in each lesson for direct instruction is often a mandated part of lesson plan formats. Many people would assert that direct instruction is the most critical part of the lesson: presenting students with an ever-expanding collection of facts and academic skills. Some people may see the rest of this book as fluff, merely a way of socially and emotionally helping students manage the flood of information and procedures raining down on them every hour, in increasing cascades as they move from grade to grade. The most basic mandate of a teacher is simple: students enter my class not knowing, and my job is to make them know.

I certainly contributed to that cascade of academics for my students. I had them for a small part of their lives; I was given the job by the school system, and by the larger society, to teach the year's quota of the curriculum. "Clear your desks!" "Focus up here!" "Yes, this is on the final exam!" "There's no time to lose!" I may not have said all those words, but I am sure I exuded that sense of urgency. Or was I exuding my anxiety?

If only we all had such power over our students, to gain their unwavering compliance simply by demanding it. Actually, it's just as well that we don't, because then our precious, diverse, ever-evolving, delightful students wouldn't be real humans. They'd be robots that resembled students, programmed to march in and out of our rooms, their android eyes fixed on us, the proverbial empty vessels awaiting our downloads of facts and procedures, later uploading their hard drives into the central computer that periodically administers standardized tests to see that they are functioning properly. That description certainly sounds like a more manageable teaching job— if humans were robots.

I hope you chuckled, thinking of students as compliant robots. We adults know that's not what we think of them. But sadly, many of our students begin to feel like featureless machines with every passing year, the feeling accelerating through middle and high school. By their senior year, only 59 percent of students say school inspires them to learn, only 54 percent say their teachers make an effort to know them, and only 36 percent say that teachers make school an exciting place to learn (Quaglia & Corso, 2014). We may not think of students as learning robots, but the institution of school engenders such feelings in them through 12 years of relentless curricula.

The concept of teaching whole humans doesn't get better for students who go to college. The brain science that informs us of the interaction of cognition and emotions is often of little consequence in higher education. Long lectures remain a predominant means of pedagogy; students are expected to provide almost all of the motivation for learning, techniques for learning, and capacity to wrangle their lecture notes into deep understanding. That is not the formula for robust education, and we should not be replicating it in any K–12 classroom! Nearly one-third of first-year college students drop out (EducationData.org, n.d.). Preparing students for bad teaching in college by providing them with bad teaching in our K–12 schools is unethical, as well as substandard.

I must pause here to identify a notable difference between the work of early elementary teachers and all the teachers who follow. Perhaps that difference can be best summed up by a high school teacher who confided in me, when told his work now included SEL goals, "I'm not getting out mats and graham crackers for my students! Early elementary teachers do that! I don't have the time with the curriculum I am given!"

I have heard for years that the curriculum is the problem as students get older: there's too much of it, and not enough students have the prerequisite skills and knowledge to succeed. Unfortunately, now I am hearing the same concern from early elementary teachers. They clearly still have more room to be playful—to be "whole people"—with the little kids, but the pressure is growing on them to limit the bountiful learning of play, learning that seamlessly integrates the cognitive, social, and emotional growth of children, in order to make more room for explicit direct instruction.

This chapter is going to help you make sure your SEL goals and the SEL goals the students hold for themselves will be part of the critical experience of providing and receiving direct instruction—at all grade levels.

Why Direct Instruction Needs SEL

"Direct instruction" is not a pejorative term. We can provide direct instruction while being playful, wise, demanding, caring whole adults, engaged with whole students of *any* age. The research in brain science is robust in describing how, even during the seemingly mechanical process of direct instruction, students will be far more effective learners when we see them as whole people, when they are prompted to integrate their SEL skills. As Immordino-Yang (2016) notes:

> In the context of schools, emotion is often considered ancillary or secondary to learning, rather than an integral part of the knowledge being learned. We expect children, for example, "to get their feelings out of the way" so that they can focus on their studies.... However,... neuroscience is revealing that rather than working to eliminate or "move beyond" emotion, the most efficient and effective learning incorporates emotion into the cognitive knowledge being built. (p. 98)

Action Steps

Referencing the Essential SEL Skills chart (Figure 1.1) and a recent lesson plan, answer the following questions:

- Which SEL skills do your students need so they can effectively receive your direct instruction?
- How many of your students regularly exercise those SEL skills when they are receiving direct instruction?
- In what ways do you see and hear students engaging SEL skills during direct instruction?

Needing to exercise SEL skills to effectively receive direct instruction is where humans differ from robots. The human brain will filter out the input that doesn't rise to the "need to know" threshold; only when the input matters do our neural networks get activated to pay attention. We literally have to care to learn (Immordino-Yang, 2016).

Here is a classic example of the difference between a robot and a human trying to learn from direct instruction: during the making of the original *Star Wars* film, the actor Harrison Ford was reading the poorly written dialogue for the day's shoot—essentially the content of direct instruction from writer/director George Lucas. Ford, so frustrated by Lucas's inability to craft dialogue that matched the ways humans actually talk, shouted at Lucas, "George! You can type this s***, but you sure can't say it! Move your mouth when you're typing!" (O'Connell, 2017).

With all the attention the film gave to its groundbreaking robots, Ford wanted Lucas to care about the human actors. He wanted Lucas to have the experience of speaking the dialogue he wrote before asking others to do so. If our students could be so bold, they might say, when we demand their attention for direct instruction, "Teacher, please tell me why *you* care about this before asking me to care! I can't pay attention without *you* caring first! And if I can't pay attention, I can't learn! Don't you remember what it was like to be a kid?"

I remember when I did not know enough to integrate SEL skills into direct instruction. Deep inside, as I drove my students to the edge of their capacity to remember facts that few cared about and procedures that many were not ready to make sense of, I felt as if I were losing part of what made me want to work in schools. My SEL goals for myself as a teacher, as a human, were being washed away. I could "teach" it, if that meant I stood in front of students and made pronouncements, but few were going to actually learn it. Teaching students content and skills they didn't care about was drudgery for my students and ultimately a waste of my time, too.

I decided I had to tell my students why the facts and skills that were the heart of the lesson mattered to *me*. I had to come up with better justifications than "Your teacher next year will want you to know this" or "It's on the final exam." Yes, those prompts work for a few students, but not for enough of them, given the time we put into planning and implementing our lessons.

Action Steps

Considering a recent lesson plan, answer the following questions:

- What do *you* believe is truly important about the content and procedures of the direct instruction in this lesson?
- In what ways do you currently share with your students your beliefs about the importance of your lessons?
- Which of your students might benefit from hearing your beliefs, in order to raise the content of the direct instruction to the "need to know" threshold?

Figure 4.1 lists many reasons teachers have for being committed to the facts and processes they wish to transmit to students in direct instruction.

Action Steps

Referencing the lesson plan you've been working with, answer the following questions:

- Which of the prompts in Figure 4.1 could motivate your students to pay attention during the direct instruction part of this lesson?
- Which of those prompts do you already explicitly share with students?
- What other prompts might you explicitly share with students to raise the lesson to a "need to know" status?

FIGURE 4.1

Reasons Teachers Can Give for Direct Instruction

- I just love these ideas, and I'm excited to see and hear what you think about them.
- This lesson will help you with your friendships, because...
- This lesson will help you with your family, because...
- This lesson will help you be a better neighbor, because...
- This lesson is going to fill you with wonder; the world will seem more interesting!
- This lesson is going to spark every student to think wonderful ideas.
- This lesson will help you be a better student, because it will challenge your (concentration, risk taking, listening).
- This lesson will let each of you choose a strategy of your own and experiment, and I love watching you make decisions.
- This lesson will help you make more sense of the world and help you change the world for the better, because...
- This lesson is filled with facts that you will use for the rest of your lives.
- I've never forgotten when I learned this lesson, because...
- There is a reason this lesson is required, and that is...

The 100 Repetitions

A teaching colleague and I were talking about her frustration with a handful of students who just didn't seem to care; their lack of attention, especially during direct instruction, was causing her to feel unusually impatient. We chatted about the brain research on paying attention, and I wondered with her what would happen if she shared *her* enthusiasm for the direct instruction in her coming lessons.

Her first response was that these students had long ago stopped caring what teachers thought was important. They weren't going to suddenly care just because she made a little speech. "Oh," she said, giving me a wry smile, "this is when I might have to do something 100 times to make a difference, right?"

The "100 repetitions" is a theory that students don't magically change—they grow (Benson, 2012). They grow as a result of spending a lot of time with persistently caring adults who provide them with supports to meet the challenges of school. My colleague's most disinterested students may have needed to be prompted 100 times by her enthusiasm before they could trust her, before they would link her lesson to their own goals—goals that are prerequisites for learning.

Trust in a teacher has to be earned, especially in settings laden with historical inequities, with haves and have-nots, with teachers who aren't affiliated with the family and community cultures of their students. "This is important to learn" is a statement infused with the teacher's beliefs about the society we live in and the role these children may one day play as adults in that society.

The "need to know" prompt in the direct instruction part of lessons is important for all students, but it may be especially critical for those who are less privileged, because the playing field is significantly tilted toward those who already fit in, those members of the dominant white culture. My students who do not perk up when I say, "This is important to learn" may not yet trust that I know who they are; centuries of neglect and oppression are evident in our classrooms. I have to remember that "This is important to learn" depends on the listener's context. I may need to let my least trusting students know 100 times that I have considered who they are in elevating my lessons to a "need to know" status.

Many prompts that students hear in schools are embedded in an implicit focus on the importance of individual success, versus the collective progress of a community; that is why it is so much more common to hear in schools, "You will get ahead by learning this" versus "You will be more helpful to your family and community by learning this." The belief that tolerating the boring parts of lessons will ultimately result in financial and social success for an individual is embedded in the goal of delaying gratification through years of compliance until graduation. Many students do not see a direct line between paying attention to lessons in school and their individual long-term success in society, given its current inequities. We can strive to make explicit the benefits of a lesson in order to be of service to family, community, and society—and to help make that society more equitable. It may be we adults who need 100 repetitions to fully understand what is meant by "This is important to learn."

Action Steps

Consider the following questions:

- If you are working with a textbook or a standardized curriculum for the direct instruction in a lesson, in what ways (implicit or explicit) are students prompted to "need to know" the content?

- In what ways do your own prompts to learn the content and procedures of this lesson reflect a particular cultural perspective about "need to know"?

- What prompts during direct instruction might capture the attention of those who don't hold your perspectives on what they will "need to know" in life?

- What prompt can focus this lesson on the long-term benefits to family, community, and society?

Determining the Frequency of SEL Prompts

My conversation with the teacher mentioned earlier included another topic. She asked, "Do I have to do these prompts every day?" As always, the answer is that there is almost nothing you have to do every day. We have to consider how often we can honestly be enthusiastic about the content of our direct instruction. How often do our students benefit from our prompts before even those become another repetitive aspect of their daily experience? Which students may need prompts more than others to harness their SEL goals to the lesson?

For some teachers, the suggestion to prompt SEL skills in direct instruction will be one of the critical tools to take from this book. For others, the most useful SEL moments in their classrooms will be when students first walk into the room or during the Do-Now, as discussed in earlier chapters, or during the many opportunities we still have to uncover in the next chapters. If we consider again the notion of 100 repetitions, each SEL prompt you integrate into your lessons, and throughout the day, will help students grow in the development of new SEL skills.

Why Lecturing Is Rarely Good Pedagogy

There are times when we want to tell students of any age new information, which is why lecturing is often a big part of direct instruction. Of course, "telling is not teaching." Words alone, not tied to feelings, meaning, or experiences, will drift from our memories like untethered helium balloons into the sky, never to be retrieved again.

Simply put, lecturing is rarely good pedagogy. The human brain needs to actively participate in sense making and in linking new ideas and facts to prior learning. The extraordinary amount of lecturing at the college level is *not* the epitome of teaching and learning. Implicit in the college model is the expectation that students will spend hours outside of class trying to figure out what to do with what the professor said. We should not model bad instruction with the excuse that we are getting our students ready for higher education. That excuse diminishes the growth and learning of so many, and it caters only to those who have the external supports, specific interest in the subject, abundant time to review, prior knowledge, and well-honed self-teaching strategies to overcome the problems with lecturing.

In the next chapter I will present alternatives to lecturing. For the times you do want to tell students information, the following sequence incorporates SEL skills for the lecture part of a lesson plan:

1. Start with an activity from the previous chapter, "Accessing Prior Learning."
2. Share with students prompts that raise the content of this direct instruction to a relevant "need to know" status. Choose the prompts that best align with the culture and aspirations of your students. The more students can personalize the learning, the more they will pay attention and remember.
3. Share your own SEL goals for wanting them to learn the content—why it matters to *you* that students learn this information. The more you create an emotional charge to the act of teaching, the more your students will remember.
4. If your students have identified personalized SEL goals as discussed in Chapter 1, give them a moment to reflect on how they can reach those goals by paying full attention to the lecture.

The following prompts for different grade levels integrate your SEL goals and the students' SEL goals as preparation for direct instruction:

- **Grades K–3:** "I am so excited to talk with you today about some new words! You know one of my goals in life is to be able to talk to lots of different types of people, and these words help me reach my goal. These are words I have used hundreds of times. I even used one of these words when I met with the principal the first time, because I wanted him to know I was smart enough to teach all of you! I know many of you have an SEL goal of being able to share your own stories. These words will help all of you share your own stories."

- **Grades 4–7:** "Class, you know how much I love teaching new words. When I hear you all use our new words when you talk or in your writing, I know you are growing up to be influential people in your communities. Also, some of you have an SEL goal of matching the words you use to the setting you are in. A couple of these words are great to use when you want to apologize and not get in more trouble."

- **Grades 8–12:** "I am really looking forward to today's lesson. One of my SEL goals, a goal some of you share with me, is to effectively give and receive critical feedback. For me, I need a lot of thoughtful words when I talk with you one-to-one about your progress, right? Similarly, you all are learning to be effective when we are doing peer reviews. A couple of these words are game changers, helping us communicate better when we need nuance and strength, in school and out in the world."

> **Action Step**
>
> Write a prompt for the direct instruction of a coming lesson, using the models above that incorporate your SEL goals and the SEL goals of your students.

Sharing an SEL Lecture Goal

I once shared with my students my SEL plan to be a better teacher by improving my drawing skills during lectures. Truthfully, at my best, I can draw primitive stick figures. My students always loved watching my efforts to illustrate new information with crooked lines, jagged arrows, and oddly shaped speech bubbles. Many students linked their long-term learning of certain facts to the very act of watching me struggle with a simple drawing. They were rooting for me to improve, and that interpersonal connection gave the lecture meaning—which builds memory.

On the other hand, I feel confident reading aloud, and I always enjoy reading aloud to students—of any age! Although we may not get out the mats and graham crackers for our older students, many of them will appreciate hearing a good reader provide an enthusiastic rendition of everything from a poem to a chemistry textbook. Yes, this is a prompt for you secondary school science teachers, history teachers, and math teachers to put some drama into the reading of what are far too often horrifically dry textbooks. Make the "boring parts" of the lesson—for example, the reading of the textbook—a challenge for your professional growth to not be boring! Students have plenty of practice tolerating boredom; they don't need any more in your classroom.

Action Steps

Professional improvement as a teacher is an adult SEL goal that incorporates "skills for self" and "skills as a community member." With that in mind, answer the following questions:

- What professional goals do you have that will influence how you prepare for and deliver direct instruction?
- In what ways might you share those goals with your students to model investment in working on SEL goals?
- What feedback can you ask students to give you on your SEL goals so that they have a heightened focus when you lecture?

SEL Skills to Summarize Direct Instruction

Direct instruction should not last more than 10 minutes for students of any age. During that time, and definitely at the end of the instruction, ask students this question: "What seems interesting or important to you right now?" After 10 seconds of silent think time, have them turn and talk to a peer, sharing their uniquely crafted responses to the question. You can briefly remind them that the turn-and-talk allows them to practice their SEL skills of emotional self-awareness, working with similarities and differences, and communicating with others.

SEL and Note Taking

Note taking from direct instruction can and should be one of the most wonderful times in school for students of any age—a point that I will elaborate on in a moment. Here again, schools get it right with our littlest students and then progressively grind away all the play and joy from the process as students grow up. Many middle school students are completely befuddled by note taking. ("You'll need to take notes in high school and college" just doesn't seem to be much of a motivator, does it?) Many high school students believe note taking is another exercise in "guess what the teacher is thinking," as betrayed by the innumerable versions of the anxious questions "Is this what you want?" or "Is this going to be on the test?"

Let's consider the "note taking" our youngest students are asked to do when they learn a new word or science fact: they draw a picture! They are encouraged to make it personal, to make it big, to make it colorful. They connect previous learning through illustrations, as they include backgrounds and people to inhabit their drawings. The students are often sitting at tables, watching each other and being encouraged by their teachers to compare and share their work. So many SEL skills are being exercised!

The practice of two-column notes in secondary schools offers a bit of personalization during direct instruction. One column of the note paper is dedicated to what the teacher (or textbook or final exam) wants the student to know, written in prescribed phrases and words; the other column is dedicated to personalization, a space for writing metaphors, clever definitions, little drawings, graphs, rhymes, and idiosyncratic connections.

This process is the heart of how we humans really learn—by expanding the neural connections in our brains and securing new ideas to all the possibilities that are embedded cognitively and emotionally in our prior learning. Without the effort to expand on our prior learning, no new learning occurs.

By adding one more step to note taking—the SEL skills that further personalize direct instruction—my students' note taking became a special part of their expanded learning: we reclaimed the elementary school practice of sharing. I'd ask students to share their strangest ideas, their weirdest drawings (remember, I had been modeling nontraditional drawing all year), their funniest definitions, their most pointed critiques. I encouraged them to borrow and steal from each other. There were many occasions when a student's notes were so wonderful that the class insisted that I make a copy for everyone. We laughed together, appreciated together, and learned how to be better note-takers.

Collectively, the students learned to take meaningful, personalized, and therefore memorable notes. Many times, the most interesting additions to our collections came from our least traditionally competent students—the ones who had long ago stopped playing the game "Guess What the Teacher Is Thinking" but delighted in being contrary; simply put, they saw things differently, and different was memorable. In those moments, they became part of the intellectual commerce of the class, a place they hadn't chosen to step into for a long time. Everyone's SEL skills "as community members" were richly developed—as was, quite deeply, our very notion of who was included in the community of learners that made up our class.

Questions and Answers

You seem to be saying that we shouldn't tell students, "This is the boring part," because that will not help them pay attention. Isn't part of life mastering being bored? Isn't handling being bored an SEL skill?

I will start with a personal response. I hated how much I was bored in school. I got plenty of practice being bored, as I think almost everyone did. Telling me I'll be bored as a way to get me to pay attention is not a very effective pedagogical move. I'm not sure that "ability to see boredom as motivation" is in the skill set of most adults, much less children of any age.

If you are inclined to preface direct instruction with the warning "This is the boring part," let that be a signal to you to do something different! We wouldn't allow an adult to hit a child with the justification that "life is full of pain, so you might as well get used to it." A middle school friend once whispered to me, in the midst of a mind-numbing lecture, "Do you think they are getting us ready for being as bored as they are with their lives?" In retrospect, that moment has influenced my entire career in education as much as any college-level course in instructional practices.

And you are right: handling being bored is an SEL skill we can *explicitly* teach—just not as an excuse for lessons that evoke no emotion or participation. There are behaviors students can employ to manage boredom, as there are behaviors to employ during a fire drill. Lots of students get in trouble when they are bored because they don't know what to do with their mouths or hands or feet. Managing boredom is a skill we need to move from implicit to explicit instruction! Let's help them manage boredom.

Action Steps

How would you like students to manage boredom in your class? Consider the following possibilities:

- Make a list to share with your students of strategies for dealing with times they are bored in your class. For instance, if it is all right for students to doodle when they are bored, let them know that—and *praise them* for doodling when they could otherwise be disruptive.

- Ask students to add their ideas to the list. Have them choose the methods they think would work best for them. Turn a persistent conflict and disruptive element of schooling into an SEL win-win!

But what if students are doodling (or otherwise coping with boredom) during lectures so much that they miss important information?

I wouldn't worry too much if occasionally a student is doodling. If lots of students are doodling, I strongly suggest *you* revisit the options to raise the lesson to the "need to know" threshold and activate their receptors by employing warm-up activities that access prior learning. Their abundant use of the SEL skill for managing boredom is a strong message to you to adjust lesson planning—unless you also think a purpose of schooling is to prepare students to be bored adults!

There are days, even if you have prepared a well-differentiated and SEL-laden lesson that is working for almost everyone, when a couple of students may be managing a great deal of internal disruption. Doodling now and then is a good choice for staying out of trouble.

For a specific student who is chronically bored, the answer may require empathetic detective work. What is it in *these* lessons for *this* student that hasn't risen to the "need to know" level to compete with doodling? The student may be tired, hungry, anxious, or depressed. The student may have a learning disability limiting the amount of information they can hear and effectively process without a break. Perhaps the student doesn't have the fund of previous learning to support the next part of the curriculum. Perhaps the student finds the entire enterprise of school alienating and will need the team of adults in the school to hang in through 100 repetitions of caring and reaching out to break through that alienation. Let another member of the team know your concerns. See the boredom as a symptom resulting from the student's entire life, not a challenge to your pedagogy and authority.

5

Time to Experiment and Discover

In the previous chapter, we looked at best practices that incorporate SEL skills into direct instruction. Traditionally, the next step in a lesson plan is a time provided for students to practice with the new information—for example, solving a set of math problems, writing new vocabulary words in sentences, finding locations on a map, using the microscope, or shooting free throws in the gym.

The lesson plan sequence of being told information and then putting it to immediate use is clearly better than being told information and not using it. Doesn't that seem obvious? The time students spend engaging their skills should generally be the longest part of the lesson. All knowledge takes root in the actions of thinking and connecting, holding and turning, erasing and restarting, pondering and checking. We express our knowledge through skills: talking, writing, building, drawing, moving, displaying.

Simply put, we have to do some "messing about" to learn. In his wonderful essay "Messing About in Science," David Hawkins

(1965) advocates for abundant time spent in exploration and experimentation—messing about—and not necessarily as the step *after* being told information. The exploration is a great place to *start*.

The exploration itself reveals to students what they know and the questions that will lead them to understand more. "You must reach out to the world," writes Eleanor Duckworth (1996), "with your own intellectual tools and grasp it, assimilate it, yourself. All kinds of things are hidden from us—even though they surround us—unless we know how to reach out for them" (p. 7).

Understanding is more than cramming for a final test and then forgetting. Understanding comes from time spent messing about with things and from the innumerable questions, ideas, and facts that result. Long before we packed little humans into school buildings and designated that portion of their day as "learning," our species evolved to learn from interacting with the sensory world around us (Abram, 1996). Touching a rock in the hot sun raises questions about that rock and heat and the sun and our skin. We evolved to push boundaries, to see what happens, to try again, to discover which reactions fit a predictable pattern and which remain unpredictable, and, from all that activity, to understand how our current exploration fits into everything else we have come to know. Without the experience of our senses, how can we truly understand?

I have seen many teachers intuitively provide time to mess about in the simple task of asking their students to examine a class textbook or novel: look at the cover, the artwork, the chapter titles. Then these teachers provide the great open-ended prompt that is the antithesis of "guess what the teacher is thinking." They ask, "What do *you* see, what do *you* think, and what do *you* wonder now about this book?"

But what if no student were able to locate the publishing date, the SWBAT of the day's direct instruction? It's OK—because the students are poised to consider how the publishing date can shape and reshape what they have already observed. Now the simple prompt to "check out the publishing date" fits into a context that has some meaning, what students already have figured out about this book.

After students explore on their own, if you ask, "Who can tell me why it is important to know the publishing date?" the typically few students who have the "right" answer (for that is what the question is asking for) will once again raise their hands. You know already who they are; their peers do as well, and they will passively wait for you to reinforce whatever the curriculum is demanding in the moment. No SEL skills required.

Instead, consider saying, "Given all that you learned about the book so far, let's think quietly for 15 seconds. What does the publishing date of this book make you think about and wonder? I know what *I* think and wonder; I have no idea what *you* think and wonder."

This first step of messing about—examining materials—is appropriate for all subjects and for all ages. Math students can examine a sample problem displayed on the board and notice every detail, a process that enhances effective problem solving, before plunging into computation. Students in a physical education class can examine the boundaries and distances on the court or field of play and predict optimal strategies. Students can examine a map of Europe from 1920 and identify features that stimulate innumerable entry ways into understanding. A homework page closely examined allows students to consider the length of time required to complete the task, the specifics of the directions, the possibilities of working in a nonlinear fashion, the potential need for scrap paper, the prior knowledge that sparks effective problem solving. Each of these situations is ripe for the prompts "What do *you* see? What do *you* think? What do *you* wonder?"

Enhancing Exploration with Explicit SEL Prompts

We are learning creatures. I wish our schools more intentionally protected and affirmed that precious human characteristic in every interaction, in every administrative decision, in every standardization of the curriculum, and in every schedule and budget calculation. The imperative to have all students learn the same skills and content in a course of study should be matched by the imperative that they all leave that course of study with an affirmation of themselves as lifelong learners.

"Most developmental psychologists believe that a child's need to know is a drive as pure as a diamond and as distracting as chocolate" (Medina, 2009, p. 273). We need to recover in all children the inherent joy of discovery and the excitement of having their own wonderful ideas. Choice helps, think time helps—and crucially, so does teachers' unbridled curiosity about the idiosyncratic journeys taking place in their students' brains as they explore, experiment, and mess about. This is where SEL has to be an intentional part of the lesson plan.

Prompts that repeatedly reveal our heartfelt desire to honor how each student constructs knowledge—both during explorations and as students share their discoveries—allow the exercise of many SEL skills, including the following:

- **Emotional self-awareness.** The expression of feelings is not limited to therapy. Talking about what personally has meaning in the curriculum definitely makes learning stick! We set the stage for students to express their "aha" moments of personal discovery—which can also come from correcting errors in the midst of an exploration. Our emotional responses to their discoveries can range from a quiet nod of the head to high fives to a loud cheer.

- **Identifying strengths and supports.** Everyone is capable of seeing, thinking, and wondering, all from their own strengths. When we affirm a student's contribution to the class exploration —for example, by saying, "What a wonderful idea! You made the connection between the artwork and the age of the book, and I never thought about that!"—the student develops a sense of personal competence.

- **Working with similarities and differences.** One aspect of opening up the curriculum for all to uncover and discover is the range of responses the class gets to enjoy and be challenged by. I have worked with many students who almost never volunteered to answer a right/wrong question, but with encouragement (perhaps 100 times!) and their evolving trust in the safety of the class, these students told us ideas from their explorations that startled us and expanded our understanding. Such opportunities are especially important in our efforts to include all voices from all communities and cultures in our schools. The experiences of students who come from families with a long legacy of confronting racism, and the experiences of all students who have encountered prejudice, can be curriculum content that informs us all.

- **Contributing to the greater good.** As students realize that we really are interested in what they think and wonder, the sharing of ideas is ultimately about making a contribution. Surely one of the goals of our educational system, somewhat obscured by the dominance of standardized tests and report cards, is to foster the expectation for students to use what they learned in schools to be contributors in their communities.

Here's how SEL prompts can sound as the class shares what they have discovered after a period of exploration:

- **Grades K–3:** "Friends, think for a moment. What is the most wonderful thing you noticed when you were mixing colors?

We are going to have a chance to listen to each other's ideas. When we listen to each other after we have experimented, we learn so much about how each of us discovers things. When it's your turn to share, you will get stronger at talking and you will help us all get smarter. And I know that for some of you, a special goal is to learn from what your friends share."

- **Grades 4–7:** "It's time to share and hear what you discovered when you were measuring the size of those objects. This is a time when it's OK to be excited about what you found out—to be the owner of what *you* just discovered. And the rest of us, when we are listening, get smarter by adding other people's experiences to our own. We'll make the world a better place by putting together every discovery we make in this room. And some of you have that as your SEL goal for this month."

- **Grades 8–12:** "OK, you've read an essay, read the intro to the textbook, and watched two videos. It's time to hear how each person is making sense of all this different input. If you are excited by what you think, this is your time to share—and if you are confused or angry or bored, this is also your time to share. We learn with our thoughts and feelings, from *all* of our thoughts and feelings. Isaac Newton said, 'If I have seen further, it is by standing on the shoulders of giants.' We are wiser and smarter together than alone. And if we have any hope of improving this world, which is an SEL goal for many of you, we have to start by learning from everyone in this class."

Action Steps

In the section of a lesson plan where students will be practicing, exploring, and experimenting to secure their learning, do the following:

- List the types of learning you hope students will construct from exploration that couldn't be achieved by just telling them facts and procedures.

- Choose the SEL skills that will help them get the most from this exploration and practice time.
- Craft a prompt for using those SEL skills in this lesson.

SEL Skills and Constructivism

Albert Einstein said, "I never teach my pupils. I only attempt to provide the conditions in which they learn." The notion that humans learn by directly experiencing some essential interplay with materials and ideas is the heart of the theory of *constructivism*.

Constructivism involves a dedication to classroom practices that provide the conditions for all students to do their own sense making, conditions rich in SEL skill development, as students talk, ponder and fret, refocus, share and compare their work, adjust their approaches, ask for guidance (not answers!), and lean into their evolving strengths. David Hawkins famously said, "We have to cross the boundary between knowing and not knowing many times before we achieve understanding." Deep understanding is the goal, not surface imitation of the teacher's pronouncements. For example, math manipulatives don't foster a deep understanding of fractions when the expectation is to simply re-create what the teacher has already demonstrated to the class. Students have to mess about.

The conditions for messing about are structured, not an invitation to chaos. The prompts that guide students into the exploration can include time limits; boundaries on how and where to use materials; charts and graphs to catalogue discoveries; and, of course, reminders of the SEL skills that will enhance their learning.

All the things we've explored so far in this book—choosing and sharing personal SEL goals, creating welcoming routines and rich Do-Now activities, supporting students to make sense of the SWBATs of the lesson, activating prior knowledge as a class collaboration, finding purpose and commitment to direct instruction—are structures that allow for optimal messing about. Over the years, I have found that the following steps make for a learning experience that is filled with SEL benefits. You may not need to carefully implement each step for every lesson; this list provides a look at the full exploration experience:

1. Students take in, with any and all of their senses, the lesson's artifacts, materials, worksheets, or books. Students who are old enough to write can be provided with a "See/Think/ Wonder" form to report back their observations and discoveries; teachers of younger students can solicit their contributions. The SEL prompt can sound like this: "Class, in this exploration period, while you are discovering everything you can about our materials, consider how the people around you are working in our learning space. It is up to each of us to make sure everyone has the space to be themselves, think their own thoughts, and make their own unique discoveries."

2. Students share their observations and discoveries. The SEL prompt can sound like this: "Class, this is a great time for us to hear and appreciate how different people understand the same materials from varied perspectives."

3. Now that the students have a good sense of the possibilities inherent in the lesson's materials, the teacher offers a variety of experiments, tasks, and challenges that require an intentional engagement with the materials. As we saw with the Do-Now tasks in Chapter 2, this step of discovery can offer a variety of entry points and skill levels. I often ask students to suggest their own experiments or to challenge a friend to try an experiment. The SEL prompt can sound like this: "Consider for a moment how you feel today. Is this a good day to try a task that seems really challenging? Do you feel like you can handle some frustration? Maybe this is a day when you want

to work within your current strengths and use those strengths again. Choose the task that fits your needs today."

4. Students share their processes and outcomes, including their "aha" realizations from experiments that went as planned and from experiments that did not seem to work out. During this time, the teacher is listening for the students' levels of understanding and their confusion. The SEL prompt can sound like this: "Class, we learn by trying. As we share our discoveries, I'd like you to take the risk of adding how you feel from trying. Did your exploration make it more likely or less likely that you will be excited when we mess about again? Listening to you will help me plan better, and that will be good for everyone."

5. All of the preceding steps have primed the students for a session of direct instruction, which is now focused and targeted to what the students have already revealed about their understanding and confusion. The teacher references the ideas and questions of many students, honoring their thinking and efforts. Experiments that "failed" are considered important data that build the collective understanding. The direct instruction confirms, expands, and crystallizes ideas that have already been developing through active engagement. The SEL prompt can sound like this: "Class, now that you know so much, it's time for me to focus your thinking in a couple of particular places. We will also take a moment to thank everyone whose efforts added to our learning."

Exploration Example #1: A Trip to Manhattan

Here's one of my favorite applications of "messing about" exploration. A middle school in the Boston area was preparing a class for a bus trip to New York City. The teacher, Ms. A., wanted to acquaint her students with the unique geography and street design of the city.

Students in groups of four were given a map of Manhattan, with the task of listing 10 interesting observations—a much better prompt than being told to find their hotel or the museum they were visiting, because there would be nothing for the students to do once they were told the information, nothing for that information to connect with, and no learning. Instead, given her prompt, the students plunged into the task of uncovering Manhattan, the classroom bubbling with happy and contagious chatter.

Students were asked to share a favorite discovery from their varied explorations of the map. As Ms. A. predicted, there were many remarks about the extensive grid of streets and famous places. Then one group of students told the class they had calculated the square footage of Central Park! Immediately, many students gave Central Park another long look, and a few wanted to double-check their peers' calculation. Ms. A. was not a math teacher, but she knew the class's excitement could be channeled into her lesson plan (Step 3 in the earlier list, when students are given their next challenge). She said, "Now I want all the groups to come up with one math fact about this island that you don't think anyone else will try to figure out. You can measure anything, calculate anything. Find out a number fact about Manhattan!"

Five minutes later, the class was enthusiastically sharing all sorts of trivial information about distances and areas, the highest and lowest numbered streets and avenues, the distance of the longest avenue. As each group told of its discovery, the rest of the class was guided to look at the part of the map that yielded the data.

Only at this point did Ms. A. provide the day's "lecture." She told the class where on the map to find their hotel and the museum they would be visiting. She told them the path they would take to walk between the two sites. She had them highlight the path on their map. As she told them each detail, the students were absorbed in following what she said, with an occasional student shouting, "We saw that already!"

Her SWBAT had been to promote student safety by being acquainted with the neighborhood in Manhattan where they would be staying and walking. The information in her lecture landed in a matrix of understanding that had been richly developed in the previous 15 minutes. The class was hanging on her every word, as opposed to passively listening to a lecture, with no personal interest in the information—that is, minimal learning.

I saw Ms. A. the day after the class's return. She said, "What most impressed me was how the students were talking as the bus entered Manhattan. They were calling out to each other the sites and streets. They were anticipating where the bus would be passing, and moaning when the bus turned down a different street. You would have thought that they had once lived there. I suppose they did, in their heads."

Action Steps

In the scenario about the class trip to Manhattan, Ms. A. never explicitly references SEL skills. With that in mind, do the following:

- List specific SEL skills that were essential for this successful learning experience.
- For one part of her lesson, craft an SEL prompt that would raise those skills to an explicit and intentional level of practice.

Exploration Example #2: "Inventing" a Math Process

One of the most startling discovery explorations I have learned about is from a group of 5th and 6th grade students, inventing the complicated process for dividing a fraction by a fraction (Warrington, 1997). The students had been exploring all year in class; their teacher, Ms. W., relentlessly guided them through the process of exploration and invention. She trusted them to want to understand math (what a refreshing attitude!) rather than become baffled by its increasing complexity.

Ms. W. started this ambitious exploration by asking her students questions that accessed their prior learning regarding fractions and division. She carefully began to ask questions that led them into experimentation and exploration ("What if the second number was ¾?"). The students accepted her challenges while self-correcting, listening to each other, questioning each other, and affirming each other—SEL skills in full bloom! She never said in absolute terms, "You are right" or "You are wrong," but instead provided the class with another challenge that supported explorations of their own hypotheses: would those hypotheses hold up to further scrutiny? The truth did not lie in Ms. W., but in the results of the students' explorations.

The key moment in their collective invention of the division algorithm came when one student had a hypothesis that contradicted what everyone in the class had assumed was true: "She was a child standing alone, disagreeing with an entire class of peers," Ms. W. observed. The class asked Ms. W. which was the right answer. To tell them an answer then, when they were so socially, emotionally, and cognitively engaged, would have ended their thinking and learning and shut down the innumerable parts of their brains that were lit up. Instead, she gave the class a new prompt that allowed them to explore this girl's singular idea: the students' job was to come to a conclusion about this new hypothesis. In this way, she honed their SEL abilities to communicate understanding of another person's perspective, to work with their strengths and emotions, to admit mistakes, and to assess how their actions affect others. Her students may have needed 100 repetitions of her not giving them an answer before they knew how much she trusted them to work harder and deeper as a class searching for the truth.

"The debate resumed. This sort of intellectual bantering amongst children is a desirable and typical occurrence in a constructivist classroom. It is a processing of ideas which results in deeper understanding... *social interaction is absolutely essential to the construction of knowledge"* [emphasis added] (Warrington, 1997).

Action Steps

In the two exploration scenarios, the traditional sequence of providing direct instruction before guided practice is reversed: Ms. A. waits until the students have fully explored their Manhattan maps before her lecture, and Ms. W.'s "direct instruction" comes in the form of prompts and questions, allowing the students themselves to uncover and confirm the lesson's SWBATs. With this in mind, consider the following:

- What SEL skills would you want to explicitly prompt and reinforce with your students to allow for such extended and open-ended exploration?
- Like many teachers, you may fear that students' frustration in a long exploration will outweigh their creativity and excitement. Craft an SEL prompt that supports your students to manage temporary frustration, so that managing the emotions of learning becomes part of your class culture.

Options and Ideas for SEL-Rich Explorations

The SEL skills that teachers prompt, model, and reinforce are absolutely essential to the construction of knowledge. The exploration portion of the lesson plan—the time to mess about with peers under the teacher's guidance—taps into how we are truly built to understand.

You can implement the options and ideas described in the following sections with or without first providing direct instruction. The intent is to make your classroom and your lessons exemplars of teaching the whole student, where the integration of SEL skills and the active construction of knowledge through exploration are not only the norm, but also an affirmation of the science of how people truly come to understand. I am happy to see more of these practices, so common in elementary schools, being implemented in secondary schools.

SEL and the Choice to Work Alone or with Others

My nephew plays on his school soccer and basketball teams and is an exemplary teammate. In those contexts, he demonstrates sophisticated levels of SEL skills: he adjusts his behavior to the setting, develops plans to meet goals, recognizes his teammates' nonverbal cues, admits to his mistakes, and initiates actions to help his team succeed.

But when he is in the classroom, he prefers to work on his own. When his teachers insist on pairing students or putting them in groups, he almost always asks to work solo. Teachers rarely agree to that request. When they tell him, "You have to learn to work with others," he sighs in silent exasperation and complies. "But I know what works for me," he'll say later, "and that is being at a desk by myself, figuring things out in my own way."

As a teacher, I asked my students to give me the names of three students they'd like to sit with to do their best work ("smart seats") and three students who might not be great partners for academics but with whom they are friendly ("social seats"). Their choices helped me to craft seating charts, and to pair and group students for assignments.

Because seating really means a lot to students within the daily social cauldron of schools, my students were highly motivated to convince me to comply with their requests for work partners. I prompted them to be effective in convincing me by explicitly reminding them to exercise their SEL skills of identifying their feelings, making plans, identifying their strengths, and matching their behavior to the setting of our classroom.

My students had the explicit right to advocate for changes in my seating decisions, which always led to wonderful conversations that exercised their SEL skills; after all, they were sure their choices would promote the greater good: "Mr. B., being with this student will make me calmer, and you said that helps brains function, and you want me to advocate for my needs based on my strengths, and the whole class will be quieter if I am focused on my work, and that will be good for you too!"

Their impassioned speeches always made me smile but did not always lead to permanent changes in my thinking or plans. Quite often I would say to pairs of students, "I think you two sitting together will be far more a social seat than a smart seat! Let's make a deal. If this is truly a smart seat, when I come by your desks in five minutes, what will be accomplished? What evidence will there be that this is a smart seat?"

They had to make plans to meet that five-minute goal; if the evidence was there, I was willing to admit they were right and I was wrong. I truly wanted them to be right, proving that they could make plans, work from strengths, develop solutions that account for varied needs, express their feelings respectfully, and predict the outcomes of their actions—a bounty of SEL development.

One of my all-time favorite outcomes of this process was when I granted two very rambunctious boys the opportunity to work together ("You two *really* think this will be a smart seat?"). Within a minute, one of them called me over as his buddy was having a giggling fit and said to me, "Get me away from him, Mr. B. This is totally a social seat!" What a perfectly wonderful moment of deep SEL growth!

Students know much about how they can work best. We should offer them multiple opportunities to explore working with others, so they can exercise and expand their SEL skill set. But I feel strongly that we need to honor students who want to mess about alone, or only with one or two other specific students, and then use that time effectively to meet the SWBATs. They are demonstrating their SEL skills of emotional self-awareness, personal goal setting, and identification of strengths, and they deserve our praise and support.

SEL and Memorization

There are times—and not just "for the test"—when teachers want students to commit a fact or procedure to memory. Explicitly being tasked to mess about with memorization techniques allows pairs and small groups of students to brainstorm ways to memorize. They then experiment to find the techniques that work best for this content, simultaneously building their foundation of facts and their executive function tool kit.

But first I must offer a caution about memorization tasks. The facts we want students to recall have to fit into a mental schema, into their prior knowledge, into a framework of meaning. Perhaps we need a different word than *memorizing* to honor the emotional and cognitive processes that must intertwine to recall information. Brains need to make a coherent story out of a set of facts for the facts to achieve permanence, a story we can elaborate through repeated use and connections (Medina, 2009). Even the driest facts require a personal journey of construction—some messing about—to become part of us.

I struggled as a teenager when I was required to memorize the mathematical order of operations; the string of initials given to me (PEMDAS) seemed so random. I kept looking for a logic to it, a schema that would embed it into my understanding and make it stick. Then I learned that there was no absolute logic to it—at some point, mathematicians simply had to agree to an order so they could follow each other's work. I remember laughing aloud. I had found my path to memorization; I had a personal narrative of exploration that gave PEMDAS a special meaning to me.

You can prompt and reinforce the following SEL skills for explorations related to memorization: using words to identify feelings, identifying one's strengths, developing solutions that account for varied needs, and advocating for needs and resources.

SEL and Workstations

Similar to the approach of providing varied Do-Now options, described in Chapter 2, students of all ages can move about the classroom to explore workstations, each station allowing interactions with the content using multiple entry points. The knowledge students construct as they explore the SWBATs at stations can be more complex and integrated than the outcomes of lectures. As with Ms. A. in the Manhattan map story, a rich bit of messing about can focus and minimize the time spent lecturing students. As a result of messing about in the stations, students will already be alive with the possibilities inherent in the content.

Station work exercises so many SEL skills: using words to describe feelings, identifying one's strengths, recognizing peers' nonverbal cues, working with similarities and differences, and matching one's behavior to the setting. As students begin station work, add a very explicit SEL prompt for any of those skills, and you will increase student attention to putting those skills to use and allow yourself to positively redirect off-task students by cueing them to use that SEL skill.

SEL and Making Mistakes

Among others, a great benefit of exploring materials and ideas with peers is that students observe each other making mistakes, and they then can collaboratively find solutions. Simply put, teachers rarely model being wrong in lectures: we solve all the math problems correctly on the board, demonstrate exactly where to put a semicolon, hold the instruments with the correct posture. We don't explicitly and intentionally spill liquids, break straws, or overheat test tubes.

Students do need teachers to model how skills look when done well, and then they need each other to stumble along toward mastery, away from the relentlessly evaluative eye that adults have turned on them throughout their years in school. The human brain grows more neural connections when correcting errors than it does when repeating what it already knows (Bryner, 2007)! Messing about is messy, and rethinking how one got into a mess and how to get out of it is invaluable for learning.

You can prompt and reinforce the following SEL skills for celebrating the good that comes from catching and correcting mistakes along the path to understanding: identifying strengths, advocating for needs and resources, admitting mistakes, developing solutions that account for varied needs, matching one's behavior to the setting, and identifying opportunities to make a positive impact.

Here are examples of how the SEL prompt for working with errors can sound in the different grades:

- **Grades K–3:** "Friends, I am so excited today because you are all going to have a chance to fix things! When you do today's task, almost everyone will make a mistake. You will try something that doesn't work. And then, with your friends, you will figure out how to fix your mistakes. When one of you has an idea for how to fix something, please say, 'I have an idea for how to fix that.' Some of you have a goal to listen better, and by listening to each other's ideas in this lesson, your brains will get so big!"

- **Grades 4–7:** "Class, this is one of those days when you have to explore and be ready to make mistakes. You all know that our brains grow by fixing mistakes. You will get to exercise very important SEL skills when you and your peers correct mistakes together: you will listen to each other's different ideas, find a common way of understanding the problem, and develop a solution that everyone can agree with. You might say, 'Well, the only thing we learned from that experiment was to not try that again!' But I expect your brains will usually find a way to improve your understanding, based on that experiment that didn't fully succeed. And some of you have an SEL goal of admitting mistakes. Well, all of you will get a chance to work on that goal today!"

- **Grades 8–12:** "My dear students, it's time to explore and mess about! Today's task has a few very interesting possibilities; there is definitely more than one way to complete the task. The only way you will truly learn deeply and gain wisdom is by trying, making errors, rethinking your strategy, and trying again. We've talked a lot in this class about diversity and listening to how other people see the world. Take that mindset into this lesson: how does each person make sense of what you have done? Some of you have a personal SEL goal to not only listen to someone who has a different opinion than yours but also communicate that you actually understand what the other person is saying. I think that goal is one we can all focus on today. What I can guarantee is that when you make mistakes and fix them, your brain grows new neural connections."

SEL in the Content Areas

The pedagogy of experiments is not limited to science lessons. What follow are examples of prompts in a variety of subject areas to communicate your desire for students to mess about while exercising SEL skills:

- **Language arts:** "Write up to five different ways that word could be spelled. Pick which spelling you think might be the right one. I'll want you to tell me how confident you are in your choice. You don't have to be right, and I don't want your feelings of being uncertain to prevent you from making choices."

- **Social studies:** "Go online and find five different maps you could use for illustrating that report. Think about what information is highlighted in each map. Your job as a report writer is to understand that different people will notice different details in each map. What maps might work best for your audience?"

- **Math:** "It's time to do estimation exploration. Looking at the problem on the board, what are three different ways you could estimate the answer? Which way might come up with the closest answer? You have to do that a lot in life—predict the outcomes of your actions. We do a lot of estimating in life based on assumptions, and we use those estimations to make decisions. Sometimes the assumptions are based on prejudice and not on the actual facts in front of us. Math is a great place to examine your assumptions, your estimations, and your actions."

- **Art:** "Make a quick sketch of the scene using three different vanishing points. What do you like about the possibilities in each sketch? Then ask your neighbors to tell you which they prefer. This will be a chance to listen to how the small design decisions we make in art provoke different feelings in people."

- **Physical education:** "In your group, try three different ways of getting the ball to that spot. What are the strengths and weaknesses of each strategy? And how do those strengths and weaknesses match up with your team's strengths and weaknesses? You'll have to be honest with each other about what you are good at and where you are worried you won't perform well. Athletes use their feelings about themselves a lot to prepare for competition."

Questions and Answers

What if students always want to work alone when the class is messing about? Won't I be reinforcing their sense of isolation? Isn't that bad for their SEL development?

There is a difference between introversion and isolation, between needing less external stimulation to concentrate and being scared to interact, and between knowing how to work effectively and being depressed.

Students' requests to work solo are not in themselves a symptom of anything pathological. You can observe these students through the rest of their day to see if they have age-appropriate interactions in other settings, and check in with other staff who work with them.

If these students are producing solid academic work on their own, then they are probably not overwhelmed by internal distress that would undermine their performance. In fact, they might find academic work to be soothing, an island of calm competence in a stressful day.

You can find a quiet moment, outside the hearing of other students, to ask each of these students if they would like you to support them in working with others. You can ask if there are any specific students who would be good partners. Just by asking these questions, with no expectations for any answers in particular, you are communicating to the students that you notice and that you care. Let the students know that they can get back to you on this topic any time they want, if they wish to run an experiment in working with others. And let them know that, in the meantime, you will support them working solo as long as they are being productive.

If your concerns for these students continue, then definitely be in touch with adults at their home and with your school counseling service. Helping a student cope with social anxiety requires a team approach, not a random demand by one teacher.

I understand that students can learn interesting things by messing about, but don't many students need to be directly and explicitly taught SEL skills?

If you've read this far into the book, I hope you see how many opportunities exist within the typical academic curriculum to build SEL skills. The premise of this book is that most teachers do not have the time, explicit permission from supervisors, or appropriate resources to teach SEL skills as a separate curriculum.

The vast majority of students I have worked with came to classes with some competency in every SEL skill we want children to demonstrate. Our modeling, prompts, opportunities for practice in the ongoing standard curriculum, and reinforcement and praise for using those skills do the bulk of the teaching. When the adults in the room are clear about what skills they value, model those skills daily, and consistently (if not relentlessly) make using those skills an explicit part of the class culture, those skills will become part of the character of the students.

But there are outliers for sure, the students who seem to use SEL skills only when reminded to—and even then with limited competence. These are the students who may need some explicit skills training. They'll need to be in a setting where they are able to listen, to share, and to role-play and practice. They'll need more personalized and explicit reminders to use their skills—for example, a teacher walking to their seat and providing a quiet, personalized prompt before the prompt is given to all the other students. They'll need more praise for their small demonstrations of success.

Often a lack of SEL skills will trigger a disciplinary action. The restorative justice movement has been a strong force to shift discipline away from rigidly applied punishment (as if adults can punish students into acquiring different skills!). Those who implement restorative justice teach new SEL skills while building connections, crafting restitution and apologies, and identifying structures that can reduce the chance of a reoccurrence. Restorative justice compels adults to respond to student behavior with the full set of tools that schools have as social and educational institutions. Students don't "get away" with anything. They are compelled to reflect, restore, and learn—and that learning is rich in SEL skill development.

In the absence of a strong restorative justice movement in schools, I have found that many teachers require students who have misbehaved (and whose behavior is often a demonstration of a deficit in SEL skills) to see them at lunch or after school in some form of detention. I can think of no better time to work one-to-one with a student on an SEL skill. The teacher and student can talk through the skill, role-play how the student will use the skill within the class, and make a plan for prompts, reinforcement, and checking back in. Reoccurrences of the problem behavior will decrease if "detention" becomes synonymous with explicitly working on SEL skills.

6

Formative Assessment

Watch parents teaching their children an essential task of growing up: tying shoelaces, brushing teeth, riding a bike, putting away groceries, washing the dishes. Before that day, the children have been randomly observing older members of the household perform those tasks, often on a daily basis, and therefore have a broad and deep accumulation of prior learning. The time has come for the parent to intentionally teach the children the task at hand; the parent has an explicit SWBAT.

On that day, the parents may preview and model the steps of the task—a little direct instruction—or have the children do a part of the task with them; perhaps the parents closely observe the children trying the task on their own. The parents offer suggestions in the moment for doing the task more effectively. Depending on the children's relationships with the parents, the suggestions help or hinder the learning process for the children. Ultimately, the children have to take ownership for constructing this skill set, for making it their own.

This universal model of parenting continually integrates teaching and assessment; it's all happening at once. We see the same paradigm when children learn to play sports, work in the yard, cook meals, and use tools such as screwdrivers and handsaws: the adult watches, comments, and watches some more, looking for signs that the child has reached a threshold of independent mastery. In schools, we label this in-the-moment process of providing feedback "formative assessment."

Finding the Joy in Formative Assessment

Unfortunately, a problem of scale occurs in providing formative assessment in schools. Most schools have too many students to allow personal, specific, and timely feedback to every child. Almost every day, teachers are required to present the same content to a large group of children simply because those children were born in the same year—as if on March 4 every 3rd grader is equally prepared for page 47 in the workbook—and then we judge the students' intelligence, motivation, and character based on how well they conform to such a predetermined schedule of instruction. No parent says, "Well, my first child learned to ride a bike when she was 5 years, 4 months, and 12 days old, so I'm going to expect every one of my children to learn bike riding on the day they are exactly that age." We would find such an inflexible intention laughable and bordering on abusive.

In schools, a required schedule of such inflexible intentions for all children is a synonym for "the curriculum." Every child this year must learn the same stuff, on the same days. The curriculum often comes with a pacing guide and deadlines, signaled by a "summative assessment": a final exam, a hands-on project, a report. Then the class moves on to the next chapter or the next unit. The individual student either "got it"—which comes with the goodies of praise and reports sent home with letters or numbers symbolizing all that the student learned—or the student didn't really get it. In any case, the class is moving on.

Within such an unnatural learning environment, formative assessment is a precious commodity, a chance to humanize a system that inclines too often to the robot notion of how humans learn. The school system and the textbook manufacturers may impose the date and content of the summative assessment, but formative assessment belongs to teachers and students, a daily opportunity to search for true understanding.

Formative assessment is the lifeblood of education and flows through the heart of SEL. Students reflect on their understanding and effort, identify what they need, communicate their needs, and participate in the back-and-forth of integrating feedback from peers and adults. The class has not yet moved on to the prescribed next thing; the class is where it should be, making sense and developing understanding.

Of critical importance, formative assessment allows teachers to delve into the *process* of how their students are learning and the depth of their understanding. In my years as a classroom teacher, I liked nothing more than the times I sat with students as they shared their thinking with me. What a privilege we have as teachers, to be given the opportunity and the responsibility of hearing a young person's mind at work, with the permission to influence that young mind! These moments of formative assessment nourish us as we nourish our students.

Formative assessment experiences, when our minds are in rich dialogue with the minds of students, are so often our most rewarding moments as teachers. I believe that all of us who headed into the profession of teaching imagined having rewarding relationships with students, using all of our skills to help them make more sense of this complicated world and their role in it. Those moments are what we came into this profession to do and, as teachers, in the most exalted notion of that term, what we long for on a daily basis. That's formative assessment.

> **Action Steps**
>
> Considering a recent lesson or unit from your class, do the following:
>
> - List the *explicit* formative assessments you used in order to know how well students were understanding the SWBATs.
> - List the *implicit* formative assessments (dialogues, close observations) you used, often during the "messing about" part of the lesson, when the students were practicing, exploring, and experimenting.

When I typed into my computer the phrase "how well the students were understanding the SWBATs," the software suggested I change the phrase to "how well the students understood the SWBATs." But the phrase "were understanding" is the correct verb tense of formative assessment—and of brain science! We are continually in the process of understanding; anything students are given to learn in class will be tested and refined through their experience inside and outside school, for years to come. The joy of our relationships with students is in intimately knowing their processes and progress in "understanding." In contrast, "understood" suggests the process is complete. That is a sobering reminder of the power summative assessment has in schools, embedded even in the algorithms of computer software.

Formative SEL Assessment Throughout the Lesson

A large part of this chapter focuses on the ways SEL skills are integrated with formative assessment of academic lessons. For now, we will consider how teachers provide formative assessment of the SEL skills themselves and how they can be more intentional in that effort.

Even without a prescribed SEL curriculum, throughout academic lessons, most teachers praise, critique, and comment on students' personal and social skills; there's always been an implicit SEL curriculum. Often, the adult feedback is reactive and nonverbal: teachers frown, shake their head, and adopt aggrieved postures. Less apparent, they provide a lot of feedback on SEL skills for positive student behavior, often given in silence as well: a smile, a nod, a high five.

In our silent feedback, we expect students to have honed the discrete skill of recognizing our nonverbal emotions, and those of their peers, all converging from so many families, neighborhoods, and cultures. Perhaps of all the SEL skills we need students to employ as members of our school communities, the one that requires students' utmost proficiency is recognizing nonverbal cues as assessments of their efforts.

If you have students who do not consistently respond to your nonverbal cues, do not immediately take it as a sign of disrespect or a lack of intelligence. Interpreting nonverbal cues can be challenging for students who come from a different culture than that of their teachers, for students with vision problems, and for students on the autism spectrum. When students are not modifying or repeating their SEL skills in reaction to your silent feedback, you need to be intentional in pairing nonverbal cues with clear verbal praise and prompts to do better.

Below are explicit verbal prompts that signal students to engage SEL skills throughout a lesson, and that can provide you with formative assessments of their abilities. Teachers typically and implicitly provide such prompts to assess students' academic understanding. For example, in Chapter 5, when Ms. W. posed an academic question to help her class uncover the division algorithm, she was also assessing the depth of their understanding; if her question did not activate them to use math skills for deeper explorations, she would ask another question.

Notice how the following mini formative SEL assessments are also prompts for students to use their skills; instruction and assessment are intertwined. The ways in which students respond to each of the prompts will give you a formative assessment of your students' SEL skills, while offering students reminders of those skills. These opportunities exist throughout the various parts of the lesson, parallel to the chapters of this book:

As students enter the classroom:
- "There are a lot of materials on the tables today. How can you be more aware of your surroundings to get to your seat?"
- "Aren't you going to say good morning to me?"
- "You seem upset. Am I reading you correctly? Can you tell me what's going on?"
- "Which of our community values do we need to focus on now as we start our work?"
- "You look like you are ready for working. Am I right? If not, let me know if you need something."

During the Do-Now:
- "I am interested in the reasons you chose that Do-Now. What sort of challenge were you looking for today?"
- "I think some of you are frustrated. If you are, take a moment to chill out and see if you can get yourself back on track."
- "I'd like the turn-and-talks to give us more specific ideas. What can you do to help out?"

When accessing prior knowledge:
- "What did you hear from another student that helped you remember something?"
- "What did you hear from another student that was very different from what you had ever considered?"

- "What can we do better—me included—to give more of you an opportunity to be heard? Do we need to show more appreciation when people take a risk by sharing?"

During direct instruction:
- "Let me know if this lecture is going too fast or too slow for you; take care of yourself as a student."
- "I shared why I think this information is important. In what ways do you think this information can help you in any of your goals?"
- "How are you doing right now? Do you feel confident, confused, happy, frustrated? Emotions are information about how our brains are working, and they can help you choose what to do next."

During "messing about" explorations and practice:
- "Pick a smart seat in the room for your work. In five minutes, how will you know if that is a smart seat?"
- "If you are stuck, what class resources can you use before you ask for my help? How can you help yourself?"
- "You and your partners don't always have to do exactly the same amount of work. Do you care if your partner seems to be doing more or less than you are doing? What will you do then?"

The prompts provide feedback to use as formative assessment. The feedback is part of an ongoing dialogue with students as they all develop their critical SEL skills. These prompts are absolutely not reserved for when students misbehave! Remember, student silence and compliance are not the epitome of SEL.

Formative assessments allow you to seek the growing edges in all students and then to prompt them to grow more. If your class has already identified individual and group SEL goals, as discussed in Chapter 1, the prompts and questions of your formative assessments can be consistently tuned to those goals, promoting growth on them throughout the year. If your students know *your* SEL goals, periodically ask them for evidence of your progress. What a powerful model you will be for this critical work!

Action Steps

Considering the current group of students in your class, do the following:

- List the SEL skills you randomly prompt at the beginning of a lesson and as praise and redirection throughout the lesson.
- Given how your students respond to your SEL prompts, which skills are your students currently demonstrating and which ones could use more reinforcement?
- Based on your answers to the first two steps, and referencing the sample formative assessment prompts on pages 115–116 as models, identify specific times in a coming lesson when you will focus your prompts, feedback, and praise to help your students expand their current SEL skill set.

SEL, Trust, and Formative Assessment

The longest part of a lesson should be student exploration—the "messing about" time of practicing and experimenting. This is the time to fully invest in formative assessment. A good question and prompt, crafted for these students in this moment of their evolving understanding, can trigger a burst of cognitive engagement. If your question stumps and confuses the students, you probably assumed they were further along in their understanding—that is formative assessment. Ask another question; find the prompt that sends them into action, or helps them confirm and deepen their understanding, or confirms your assessment of their academic development. Formative assessment helps both teacher and students grow in making sense of the curriculum.

Student engagement in formative assessment is a measure of how well *we* have been demonstrating SEL skills to gain their trust. Because we want our students to reveal not just what they can answer correctly but also what they find confusing and where they have made errors, they have to be vulnerable with us; students need to experience us as worthy of their vulnerability so they can learn. That absolutely requires trust in us.

To have those often profoundly meaningful exchanges with students that let us know their evolving thoughts and understanding, we have to set up a class culture that persistently engenders trust in the adults. Let me reiterate that notion: just because we are adults and have been granted the authority by universities and local school administrations to stand in front of young people as their teacher does not mean they automatically trust us to effectively and consistently care for them.

This notion is especially true in a society with such long-standing issues of unacknowledged racism and economic inequality. Student trust has to be earned, just as we often tell our students they must earn our trust to gain more autonomy. Our SEL skills are our tool kit for gaining student trust—for being good teachers.

Gaining student trust doesn't require you to be excessively touchy-feely if that is not your style. Consider the following guidelines to earn student trust for the critical opportunities of formative assessment. Many of these guidelines will reiterate suggestions from previous chapters. I hope at this point in the book it is clear that each moment of prompting and reinforcing SEL skills makes the next moment more likely to be successful. And each moment you have explicitly practiced your own SEL skills makes formative assessment more likely to be fruitful. Here are the guidelines:

- **Never shame students.** Always help them preserve their dignity, even when they err. Don't ask them questions in front of the class that you know they can't answer. Discipline them away from their peers. When you approach students during explorations, you want them to welcome your approach, your interest, and your probing questions.

- **Limit "guess what the teacher is thinking" questions.** Formative assessment is based on hearing what *students* are thinking. Because so much of their school experience has involved responding to questions with predetermined answers, many students will immediately try to guess what they think teachers want them to say, in lieu of what they actually are thinking in the moment. Keep the formative assessment prompts open ended and focused on process—for example, "Please show me what you've done so far. Tell me about that."

- **Explore students' moments of uncertainty.** Another way of saying this is "Don't rescue them too quickly." Imagine you have asked a student the sum of 10 + 10, and the student responds with uncertainty: "20?" The uncertainty in the student's voice reveals a soft spot in understanding, one that won't be toughened up for future use if you quickly respond, "Yes."

Instead, I have learned two wonderful responses that have led to much student growth. The first is "Are you asking me or telling me?" If the SWBAT is to develop mastery, the uncertainty in a student's voice is like sonar, telling us there is something down below to uncover. I am seeking the moments when the student's voice displays confidence, and I am alert to where the question in the student's voice reveals a need for more engagement. The second response is "Tell me more." I think those are the three most universally useful words in any dialogue with students. That phrase invites them to take us into their inner thinking, free of our assumptions and inferences. What they reveal with such an open-ended option is often invaluable information for us in helping them toughen up their soft spots.

- **Remember "100 repetitions."** You may need to very intentionally and repeatedly say, "I am really interested in what you are thinking. I know what *I* think, but I have no idea what you think. There's no answer I want other than what you are thinking about. I'm just curious right now about you." Schools are too often a culture dominated by summative evaluation; you may be the first teacher your students have ever met who expresses such unabashed curiosity about *their* minds at work. Some students may take a long time before they believe you are not trying to give them a grade in this moment.

- **Be truly curious.** Let the students' ideas guide the next question and the next suggestion for their explorations. The SWBATs should rarely be about a single end point, a single fact to be memorized. You are most often building a network of understanding and an array of habits of mind. There's so much to be curious about in those domains as students share their work. Your curiosity saves you from guessing what this student understands in the moment—and the depth of that understanding.

- **Show appreciation for their risk taking.** When you follow all these suggestions, this last guideline can come naturally. I have so many times laughed and smiled and given high fives as students shared their explorations and tentative conclusions. I have also sighed with them and sat in silence, sharing their confusion, nodding my head as I too pondered their dilemma. To acknowledge and appreciate the risks they took in exploring and sharing their explorations, you can say a version of this: "That was really interesting. I learned a lot about how you are thinking. Thanks so much for sharing all that. I really appreciate when our minds get to be in the same place. It's my favorite thing about being a teacher."

> **Action Steps**
>
> Considering the guidelines just presented, answer the following questions:
>
> - Which of the guidelines are implicitly or explicitly part of your class culture?
> - Which ones need to be explicitly introduced or need more reinforcement to produce rich formative assessment?
> - Which SEL skills can you more explicitly practice throughout the day to gain more trust and best implement the guidelines for formative assessment?

SEL, Metacognition, and Formative Assessment

Metacognition is our ability to reflect on our own thinking and, in that way, develop as learners. Standardized testing doesn't provide students and teachers with metacognitive information, only answers, but formative assessment is rich in the possibilities of helping students consider their strengths, their growing edges, and their approaches to learning. Metacognition is a path to mastery and lifelong learning, no matter what grade or subject we teach: "The ability to monitor and direct cognitive processes is critical for every learner regardless of age" (Frey et al., 2019, p. 70).

Our formative assessment moments with students can reveal their habits of mind, how they hypothesize and carry out thought experiments, and their executive functioning skills. Instead of waiting weeks and months to dive into the data derived from standardized tests, hoping to decipher in all those numbers what students were thinking as they labored on their responses, let's gain our information while students are actually thinking!

All the work you have done in engaging students' SEL skills will bear fruit and be further engaged as you help them develop metacognition. Students will be identifying their emotions, referencing their strengths, communicating their ideas, listening to understand contrasting ideas, and seeing how their thinking fits into the collective understanding of the class. These moments of engagement are often as delightful as it gets in the profession of teaching!

The following questions, which can be adapted for students of any age, will help develop metacognition:

- "When did you feel good about your efforts? When did you get frustrated? How did you deal with being frustrated?"
- "Which academic strategies would you try again? Do you feel confident in those strategies, or do you want some more practice using them?"
- "Were there times you asked for help, and if so, what made you decide then to get help? What did you try to do before you exhausted your strategies?"
- "What clues did you get from your partner(s) that you were being helpful? Did you ever get the sense that you weren't being helpful? In what ways might you do even better as a partner?"

Options for SEL and Formative Assessment of Academics

There is no single way to conduct formative assessment. Your approaches will need to take into account the time you have, the number of students with whom you want to engage, the technology you are using if you are teaching remotely, and the depth of understanding you are seeking in the lesson. In all the following options, the objective remains the same: explore the evolving understanding of students through exercising SEL skills.

Conferencing

Conferencing is the gold standard of formative assessment: you sit with individual students, or small groups of students, and explore their thinking. Your conversations allow you to pinpoint areas of growth and areas of confusion. You can ask questions that are specific to these students and then make differentiated suggestions for what they can do next. You can also appreciate their unique ideas and experiments, building their confidence and bonding with them.

A conference can be as short as two minutes or as long as there is time to explore while the rest of the class is able to independently stay on task. You can conference in the midst of their work and when students are sharing their results. Much of what has been suggested in this chapter is best done when conferencing with students.

Get the class ready for conferencing with a prompt. A good prompt will reference both academic and SEL skills. The students can be primed for conferences that are collaborative and mutually fulfilling as formative assessments. The prompts can sound like this in different grade levels:

- **Grades K–3:** "Friends, I am excited to watch you work and talk to you about your work. I don't want you to be nervous when I come by, but you can tell me if you are. I like to know how you feel when we talk. I know some of you have an SEL goal to tell me a little more often how you feel, so you can try that when I see you. You can ask me questions too. When I come to your workstation, we will get a chance to practice all of our good listening and sharing skills."

- **Grades 4–7:** "Class, while you work, I will be doing what I always do, walking around and asking questions to understand how you are doing. You know that your brains will grow, and you will get smarter, by sharing your thinking with me. You will also get to practice using my feedback and letting me know if my feedback is helpful. Some of you have an SEL goal of

asking more specifically for the help you need; you can practice that skill when I am with you."

- **Grades 8–12:** "You all know the routine: I'll be coming to talk
to as many of you as I can while you are experimenting with
your ideas. When I am with you, I need you to be honest with
me about whether my questions are helping you understand
or confusing you. Some of you have an SEL goal of communicating better with adults to get what you need, so let's work
together to make sure the feedback I give you actually helps
your explorations and helps you understand. And if I suggest
another exploration, you should tell me if that suggestion
sounds like a good one for you at that moment. If not, I need to
give you another option."

Quick Formative Assessment

A typically large class does not allow time to conference with
every student during every lesson, and not every lesson plan includes
small-group work. In such circumstances, you can circulate through
the classroom with a clipboard, tracking which students you have
spoken with while making notes on their levels of understanding.

The tracking of these conversations is important, to make sure
you are giving all students opportunities to grow with formative
assessment—because formative assessment is for all students! Obviously you need to be tuned in to the students who are struggling so
that you can help them adjust their strategies, but you also need to
be tuned in to your most academically competent students, helping
them experience their growing edges and asking them questions
that probe their metacognition and offer additional challenges.

When I work with teachers in their classes, as they walk around
the room during explorations, I am always fascinated by the questions students ask them, which reveal so much about the students'
SEL skills of self-care. I am fascinated as well by the questions

teachers ask students. What do they really want to know about the student mind at work? Do their questions get them the depth of understanding they are seeking? Do the students trust the teacher enough to share the precious and often tender commodities of their thoughts and efforts?

In their discussion of the necessity for students to craft their own questions, Rothstein and Santana (2011) write, "Everyone needs the opportunity to figure out the questions that are right for them to ask" (p. 1). This statement holds true for teachers as well. In the times you are circulating around the class, checking in briefly with one or two students at a time, you have the opportunity to ask the questions that are right for you to ask, the ones that help you understand.

Here are a few formative assessment questions and prompts for getting a quick insight into the academic and SEL progress of individual students while walking around the room:

- "Tell me more about…"
- "Do you feel really good about your work, or so-so, or are you struggling?"
- "How did you know that…?"
- "Where did you start? In what ways was that a good place to start?"
- "What would happen if…?"
- "What can you show me that you are feeling very confident about?"
- "Is there anything right now I can help you make more sense of?"

Action Steps

Considering the SWBATs of a coming lesson and the SEL status of your students, do the following:

(continued)

- Make a list of what you might be curious about as students engage in their work.
- Based on the list, craft a small number of questions and prompts that can satisfy your curiosity as you walk around the room.
- For your students who need a very personalized approach, craft an individualized prompt or question to have ready.

Bloom's Taxonomy, SEL, and Formative Assessment

The clipboard chart shown in Figure 6.1 (p. 128), filled in for a class learning about decimals, uses Bloom's taxonomy as a guide for questioning and explorations while tracking individual students' understanding and effort. (See Figure 6.2 on page 129 for a version of a table of verbs related to the six levels of Bloom's taxonomy.)

Here's how prompts can sound for different grades levels to scaffold students' risk taking when using the charts:

- **Grades K–3:** "Friends, as I walk around the room today, I have a lot of questions to ask you about your work. When I talk to you, please let me know how you are feeling about the work you are doing. Are you happy, or worried, or something else? I am going to practice my skill of listening really carefully to your ideas. I will also try to give you a follow-up task that is just right for you. Your job will be to tell me if you like that next task. Many of you have a goal of telling me what you need so you can do your work. This will be a time to tell me what you need."

- **Grades 4–7:** "Class, while you are working, I am going to be circulating, asking you about your work. The first thing I am going to do is ask you how you are feeling about your work. Are you confident? Need some support? Want a different task to try? I have all sorts of tasks to offer you. I know many of you have been identifying what your strengths are and asking for what you need. Let's work on that when I come to talk to you."

- **Grades 8–12:** "While you are experimenting, I will be asking you a couple of questions. I need you to give me an accurate assessment of your progress—both how far you are into the task and your prediction about finishing it well. This is time to work on those critical SEL skills for learning: self-assessment and expressing clearly what you need. The goal is to come up with a plan for finding your growing edge. My plan is to listen carefully, and then we'll see if my perspective on your work matches yours. We don't always agree."

The following action steps ask you to intentionally craft formative assessment questions for your lesson. With practice, you will develop a reliable tool kit of questions to assess student understanding, pointing toward further explorations. The time you spend filling out the "Notes on Individual Students" chart in Figure 6.1 will develop your ability to improvise questions in the moment as you check in with individual students.

Action Steps

For an upcoming lesson, do the following:

- Fill out a blank version of the first chart in Figure 6.1, designing a formative assessment question or prompt for each level of Bloom's taxonomy.
- For each level of Bloom's taxonomy, identify the students you predict will engage with each question and prompt.
- Craft your SEL questions and prompts to prepare students for your formative assessment inquiries.

FIGURE 6.1

Sample Formative Assessment Chart for Quick Check-Ins

SWBAT: Students will understand that the pattern of place value in decimals follows the pattern in whole numbers.

Level in Bloom's Taxonomy	Question/Prompt: Based on the Number 1.047,
Knowledge	Read the number.
Comprehension	What is the value of each column?
Application	Subtract 1/100 from the decimal.
Analysis	Explain the pattern of place value.
Synthesis	How would you explain decimals to your little brother?
Evaluation*	What is easier or harder about decimals compared with fractions? When would you choose to use each?

Notes on Individual Students			
Student's Initials	Level in Bloom's Taxonomy	Next Exploration Offered	Notes
A. G.	Knowledge	Read the number 1.147.	Still guessing more than telling.
B. R.	Comprehension	Look at the number 1.0475. What is the value of that 5?	Got this. Told him to keep adding columns to the right and reading them. He enjoyed that.
F. L.	Application	Subtract one-tenth.	Too hard. Had her work with B. R., quizzing each other.
G. G.	Analysis	Explain how the 0 is bigger than the 7. Or is it?	Too hard. Had him make the longest decimal number he could read—got to ten-millionths!
H. K.	Synthesis	None necessary	Spent time making a comic strip for her brother.

Student's Initials	Level in Bloom's Taxonomy	Next Exploration Offered	Notes
L. C.	Evaluation	Make a chart to compare decimals and fractions.	*Got caught up in designing the chart.*

*Evaluation has traded places with Synthesis as the highest level of the taxonomy among educators. I have had many healthy discussions with peers about the order of these two levels.

FIGURE 6.2

Active Verbs Based on Bloom's Taxonomy

Know			Understand		
copy	label	recall	associate	discuss	indicate
define	list	recognize	classify	distinguish	infer
describe	locate	reproduce	compare	estimate	interpret
discover	match	select	contrast	explain	paraphrase
duplicate	memorize	state	convert	express	predict
enumerate	name	tabulate	demonstrate	extend	relate
examine	quote	tell	describe	identify	summarize
identify			differentiate		

Apply			Analyze		
calculate	dramatize	prepare	advertise	contrast	order
change	experiment	produce	appraise	differentiate	point out
choose	illustrate	relate	break down	discriminate	prioritize
complete	interpret	show	categorize	distinguish	select
construct	manipulate	sketch	classify	divide	separate
demonstrate	modify	solve	compare	explain	subdivide
discover	paint	use	connect	infer	survey

Synthesize			Evaluate		
create	generalize	prepare	appraise	defend	order
combine	hypothesize	produce	assess	discriminate	predict
compile	integrate	rearrange	choose	estimate	rank
compose	invent	rewrite	compare	find errors	recommend
construct	modify	role-play	convince	grade	reframe
design	organize	substitute	criticize	judge	summarize
develop	plan	write	decide	measure	support
formulate					

A Simple Student Self-Assessment Rubric for Formative Assessment

Here is a self-assessment option that is a favorite of mine. The prompt is "Tell me the number that describes how well you know and understand the work," and the following rubric shows the options:

4—I know it so well I could teach it.

3—I feel good about it.

2—I could use more time and practice.

1—I'm confused.

Students of all ages can do this activity. I displayed a small hand-made poster of the rubric in my classroom and adapted the language only slightly for different grade levels. And the prompt is applicable to so many situations: I could ask the whole class to hold up fingers to give me a quick read of their needs, the prompt could be the first question I asked a student during explorations or as I finished our dialogue, or students could put their chosen number on a worksheet they handed in or on their homework.

Their responses were easy to confirm as I checked their work or asked follow-up questions. Although the prompt seemed to give a self-assessment of only their academic progress, it also gave me these insights into their SEL skills:

• Were they recognizing and correctly communicating their feelings?

• Did they understand their own strengths?

• Were they anxious about seeking support?

• Could they predict how I would react to their self-assessment?

• Did they see our class community as a safe environment or a hostile one?

Students' SEL skills have always been implicitly part of the rubric of formative assessment. The opportunity to explicitly and intentionally integrate SEL skills and academic growth in forma- tive assessment merely replicates what happens in the human brain as we learn: emotions, self-image, and self-expression support or hinder all of our cognitive efforts.

Questions and Answers

Why is there no mention of quizzes in this chapter, especially since lots of teachers use quizzes as formative assessment?

If by "quiz" you mean that the teacher asks a series of questions, allowing students to share their levels of understanding, and then the teacher uses that information to provide students with person- alized feedback, affirming what a student knows and offering dif- ferentiated suggestions for further explorations, that would qualify as formative assessment. If by "quiz" you mean a series of content questions that the teacher checks as right or wrong and returns to the student with a score that will be calculated into a final grade, that's not formative assessment.

Any assessment that does not engage the student in reflection, engagement, dialogue, or planning—in other words, that does not promote the student's SEL skills—is not going to be formative. And to put it bluntly, no formative assessment should be graded. In the next chapter, we will look at exit tickets, which give students and teachers everything they need to know from a quiz.

Why isn't there a chapter on SEL as part of summative assessment?

This is a book dedicated to teaching and learning. Not every- thing that happens in schools is designed for teaching and learning; summative assessment is often one of those noneducational activ- ities. Students receive a final score that goes into the feared "per- manent record." Students who do not ace the assessment (that is, most students) are often left on their own to make sense of that final score. For example, a student who receives a *B* might wonder, "Am

I not smart enough? Could I have advocated more for my needs? Was this my problem, or was my teacher not that good? Is it worth my time and effort to keep trying?" I have worked with thousands of students, and few of them have mastered all the SEL skills needed to construct worthwhile self-knowledge from a final score. A summative assessment that concludes a unit of learning and is never referenced again except to help formulate a grade doesn't fit the interests of this book.

If the content of the curriculum is in any way applicable to the rest of a person's life, more learning lies ahead. In that case, all assessment is formative, and no immutable final grade is needed—because there is truly no final grade.

7

Closure of the Lesson

I didn't discover the importance of building closure into lesson plans until late in my career. Until then, my lessons ended only when I had run out of time, and the students were as rushed as I was to shift gears for what came next. In retrospect, I realize that my development as a teacher followed the sequence of the chapters in this book.

As my career began, I knew I wanted the first moments the students came into my classroom to communicate that this was a special place—better than the hallways, better than the streets. I soon realized that the entire enterprise would be more compelling if "my classroom" became "our classroom." The students had to share with me a common vision of how we would be together and how I would use my authority for the greater good—employing all those SEL skills that I only implicitly understood and randomly supported. Classes began with greetings and a group check-in. My pedagogical skills had not yet been tested and honed through trial and error. What I knew how to do was be a nice guy. For many students, that was enough to relieve them of the fear of being shamed, which unleashed their cognitive abilities.

The next phase of my career as a classroom teacher was dedicated to improving my curriculum planning and delivery; that "devil" I wrote about in the introduction to this book loomed over me. Starting lessons with engaging activities became a requirement. I developed an array of strategies to differentiate Do-Nows and access prior learning. I learned how to more clearly break down and display directions. I expanded my methods of providing feedback. There was no doubt at this point that my students' academic learning was contingent on our collective social and emotional skills; the whole student was the unit of understanding.

The largest part of a teaching career—one that should never conclude—is assessment, particularly teachers assessing themselves. Improving my own SEL skills was critical for self-improvement: identifying how I felt about individual students and the impact of my feelings and biases on decisions involving them; working toward my personal goal of being a good teacher and learning from my errors; seeking the support of mentors to help me understand the limits of my own perspectives; and making a commitment to the students as my daily contribution to the greater good—or, as one mentor said to me as we parted, "Go out there and save democracy for another generation, Jeffrey." OK, I'll do my best.

I discovered that self-assessment is difficult in the ever-changing landscape of the classroom. What does "my best" look like? World events affect all of our priorities. The uncovering of decades of racial inequity—if not outright racism—in curriculum, funding, and hiring was cause to question so much of the status quo that informed my everyday practices. The emotional tenor of my new principal doing a walk-through shook up my attention and focus. The work was so compelling—and harder than anyone had ever been able to convey.

Looking back, sometimes I wish I had become so self-assured as a teacher that I could be immune to all of that background noise; on the other hand, to be immune to all of that background noise— indeed, to call it noise at all—is to suggest I was immune from the stimulation of reality. SEL skills do not convey invulnerability—quite the opposite. Self-assessment makes one vulnerable; my vulnerability helped me understand the reluctance of my students to share their own hypotheses, worries, and needs in an institution so dedicated to right and wrong answers.

Recurring self-assessment continued to impose itself on daily lesson plans. I wouldn't truly know the strengths and weaknesses of a lesson until I had presented it to a few different cohorts of students, while improving my anticipation of how students would react to various parts of the lesson and expanding my repertoire of personalized, in-the-moment differentiation. The devil won many bets until I had experience.

I discovered that some lessons were so well structured they could survive my fumbling about; there were others that I could only pitch when I knew the students were their most stable, when there hadn't been a lot of social drama to distract them. I became better at reading the daily mood of the class—an essential SEL skill to prevent teachers from descending into the robot vision of students, because robots don't have moods that affect their cognition! The more often I pitched my lessons to the sweet spot of my students' capacity and potential on that given day or hour, the more the students joined in. No surprise there—they aren't robots.

Investing Time in Closure

The last few years of brain research on how humans construct robust understanding and on the interdependence of emotions and cognition (Immordino-Yang, 2016) brought me to comprehending one more essential part of the learning process (and of this last chapter of the book): closure, and the critical role that intentionally closing the lesson plays in students' academic achievement and SEL development.

Historically, this critical phase of the learning process has been managed better in elementary schools, where teachers and students have the luxury—or the best practice—of investing an extra couple of minutes at the end of one lesson before moving on to the next one. In contrast, the random and chaotic closure of lessons in the vast majority of middle and high schools undermines student success.

In response to the mandates of "time on learning" and "teaching bell to bell," many secondary school teachers are literally mid-sentence when the bell rings—and then we ask for just a little more of the students' attention to copy that last note from the board, to hear the homework assignment be quickly repeated, to straighten up their desks and chairs, and to remember that various forms need to be signed by various deadlines.

Meanwhile, our students are facing the often impossible task of cramming multiple needs into a brief period of time between classes: going to their lockers, stopping in the bathroom, finding a water fountain, saying hello to a sibling or friend as they pass in the crowded hallways, and getting to the next class on time so as not to be marked late. As the bell rings to end a class and everyone jumps, any student's personal goal for understanding the lesson that just concluded is not going to easily be met—and neither will our goal of our student more robustly understanding the lesson.

As we are giving that final push of information and reminders, the class is already in motion—certainly mentally, and often physically. We might demand that everyone stay in their seats and wait to be officially dismissed, but the students are hearing sounds of other students in the hallway, and the precious time they need for taking care of their personal business is ticking away. Their brains have been hijacked by more pressing needs than that concluding bit of instruction and those final reminders. Be assured, those last fragments of the lesson, delivered in that cacophony of student brain activity, are not connecting to students' long-term memories.

The Inadequacy of Two Seconds

There is a moment in this maddening rush of transitions when many of us realize that we have probably been going too fast. This moment of realization also occurs at another transition in the lesson: from direct instruction into individualized practice and explorations. In both situations, the students are on the precipice of springing into time-limited action. In elementary schools, we have to include the moments students are gearing up for recess or lunch. Before the students rush to the door or plunge into their work, we ask this most common inquiry: "Any questions?"

I watched myself on a video ask this question to my class the moment the bell rang. My eyes swept across the room, and in literally less than two seconds, I clapped my hands and said, "OK! Get going." I had never known how little time I had actually given the students to process and respond to my inquiry. I was clearly stressed, trying to fit all of the requirements into my limited day. I may have asked if there were any questions, but *none* of my behavior communicated that I actually wanted anyone to respond. I was clearly delighted that no one spoke up.

In the two seconds my students had to respond to that classic prompt "Any questions?" they needed a set of advanced and well-honed SEL skills to slow me down in order to get their needs met:

- The self-awareness to realize, in just two seconds, that they had a concern that would weigh on them cognitively and emotionally if not addressed
- The commitment to their academic goals that required more teacher information in that moment
- The strength of self-advocacy to interrupt everyone's rushing forward
- The ability to read my mood and the mood of their peers, to know whether delaying the class had a prohibitive social cost

- The capacity to know whether they could express their needs respectfully and articulately with only two seconds of preparation
- The consideration of fitting into the class culture, if they were the only ones wanting more time right then
- The ability to predict the outcome of their actions, to consider the risk/reward possibilities
- The weighing of their actions within the greater good of their peers: whether their question might help others or was really a selfish activity, good only for their own needs in the moment

The overwhelming majority of students can't do all that processing in two seconds; few adults can. The class moved on. In the video, it was clear that I was happy to stay on my schedule, and I have no doubt many students could see I was fine with the fact that no one had delayed the group.

If you get nothing else from this book, let it be this: don't ask your class, "Any questions?" and then give them only two seconds to respond. Try this: ask if there are any questions, and then count to 10. Take a slow breath, scan the room, smile at a student or two, and demonstrate that you actually meant the question to be taken seriously.

Innumerable times since I adopted this practice, after several seconds, a student would say, "Mr. B., I do have a question." The students needed the time to process all the implications listed above. Those 10 seconds were very well used. I have grown to love the time this practice gives me to slow down as well, and to appreciate this group of students who have worked on the lesson. Those 10 seconds of closure have contributed to the development of SEL skills and created an island of calm in the ocean of stress that is too often the school environment.

Elementary school teachers and students are not immune from the stress imposed by "time on learning." A number of elementary school teachers have asked me to check with their supervisor for explicit permission when I have suggested a more intentional closure from lesson to lesson. They are concerned that they will need to explain and defend even 30 seconds of ostensibly "off-task" behavior, that they will be questioned about everything from how often they are allowing this transition processing to where that time is being taken from the standard curriculum. Quick answer: this time *enhances* the learning of the standard curriculum.

Action Steps

- Describe the explicit rituals you currently have for closure at the end of a lesson.
- Referencing the Essential SEL Skills chart in Figure 1.1, list the skills students must employ in order to get their needs met during your closure rituals.
- If there are schoolwide expectations for closure of lessons and classes, identify the ways your rituals of closure fit into those expectations.

The Academic Benefits of SEL-Informed Closure

An explicit and intentionally SEL-informed opening of a lesson is essential for student engagement. An explicit and intentionally SEL-informed time for exploration and formative assessment is essential for students to construct understanding. Of equal importance, at the closure of a lesson, an explicit and intentionally SEL-informed ritual helps secure students' understanding of the lesson, bolsters their executive functioning, prepares them for homework, reinforces their efforts to meet their academic and SEL goals, and predicts more success in the coming lessons. Closure is that important!

The ritual of closure is not a luxury add-on to a lesson, like a heated steering wheel in a car. Quite simply, we have to see closure as an intentional part of the lesson plan, not something squeezed in when there is extra time. The human brain needs a chance to consolidate understanding after a period of activity.

All the academic facts and procedures uncovered in exploration and discussed in formative assessment are still held in fragile short-term memory at the end of a lesson. The students' brains need a few well-protected moments of metacognition, moments to reflect on the key elements of the lesson, to connect those fragile memories into more secure concepts. Review time at the end of a lesson—literally refiring the neural network that was created in the initial explorations—continues the process of building long-term memory (Medina, 2009). Student learning is disrupted and frayed when teachers talk until the bell rings. The lesson has true closure only when the students complete *their* processing.

And, as always, that processing must take into account the students' social and emotional experience of the lesson in order to create and secure understanding. The whole student is still there at the end of the lesson, and recognition of that wholeness is integral to any sustained success. Human creations, ideas, and relationships—all of our learning—are emotional and cognitive achievements; indeed, social and intellectual achievements use the same brain systems that wire all of our physiological functioning (Immordino-Yang, 2016). Our students' learning is subject to flourishing or withering based on the SEL connections they achieve before they are rushed to the next lesson.

Closure, SEL Skills, and Homework

Preparing students for homework is part of the menu of closure for lessons. Given the ubiquity of homework, the expectations to assign homework, and perhaps many readers' unquestioned belief in its usefulness, homework deserves its own section of this chapter. I don't like setting students up for failure or unnecessary struggle, so best practices matter if homework is to be worth everyone's time and effort.

Homework is such an established part of the status quo in schools that the research on its efficacy has barely nudged standard practices. New teachers may have learned in graduate school that homework ranks only 88th in the list of practices that support achievement (Hattie, 2009), but few will have the gumption to bring up that research in a job interview or when they begin their careers.

In a lot of schools, assigning homework is a requirement of the lesson plan. Many veteran teachers have developed strategies to streamline the homework process as they comply with that mandate, no longer questioning whether homework leads to achievement. In some communities, the volume of homework given to students is considered a mark of rigor and high expectations.

One of the best practices for predicting success in homework comes during closure: a turn-and-talk with a peer, during which the students make sure they agree on what the actual assignment is, compare strategies, and help each other problem-solve. If you have a school or class culture of assigning homework, this two- to three-minute activity is invaluable. If you choose none of the other closure activities listed later in this chapter, a homework turn-and-talk can be your everyday strategy.

Here's how the prompt for that turn-and-talk can sound at different grade levels. In each case, the teacher highlights the SEL skills that can predict a successful exchange:

- **Grades K–3:** "Friends, one of my favorite times of the day is here: when each of you turns to your partner and talks about the homework. First, you'll talk about what you have to do for homework. I'd like you to raise your hands if you do not agree on what to do. Once everyone in the class is in agreement, I will ask you to find out if your partner is nervous about doing the homework. Being nervous may mean you are not sure how to do the work. It's OK to be nervous. I know some of you have an SEL goal of being a good friend, so listening to how your partner is feeling will help you be a better friend. We want everyone to be calm and know how to do the work when they get home. Then I will give the signal so that every pair of partners will have two minutes together to start the homework."

- **Grades 4–7:** "Class, the homework task is on the board. In the first minute of your turn-and-talk, I want each of you to look at your partner's homework notebook and make sure your partner has written the task down correctly. When you both agree that everything is written correctly, you will have two minutes to work together on the homework. When I signal that those two minutes are done, each of you will tell your partner how you plan to finish the homework. Some of you have an SEL goal of asking for help, and if you need help, your partner is there for you. If both of you need help, that's why I am here. Just raise your hands."

- **Grades 8–12:** "The first task in your turn-and-talk is to agree on what the homework is. That's the first minute. Listen to each other carefully. A few of you have an SEL goal to respectfully and directly communicate with others, and these homework turn-and-talks are a great place to build your skills, especially if you and your partner disagree. Then each of you shares your plans for when and where you will get homework done tonight. This is another chance to practice being honest. If you don't have a plan, use the time with your partner to make one. I'm here if you need my support."

Of course, all that preparation for homework needs to be in service of homework tasks that intentionally integrate SEL skills with cognitive skills. The following homework classifications provide that integration.

1. Students will work from their strengths, advocate for their needs, and invest in their plans for improvement by choosing from a menu of homework options. As discussed in Chapter 2 regarding the Do-Now task at the start of class, homework is another critical time for students to be given a choice. The students will engage their SEL skills of striving to meet goals, working from strengths, and predicting and evaluating the outcomes of their actions in choosing which homework task is best for them. Only in rare cases should students not be given a choice of homework tasks.

Choice allows all students to identify their academic needs while also acknowledging their particular challenges, and it offers them opportunities to prioritize and follow through on commitments. Many students, with increasing frequency as they get older, hold an array of responsibilities outside school. Choice also takes into account that our students live in a world of enormous inequity outside school. Some come from families and communities with easy access to tutors and other resources, whereas others may not even have internet access. With the rise in remote learning, the pervasive inequity of technology in our communities is highlighting the limitations of assigning only one homework task that is dependent on hardware, software, and connectivity. When we demand a single way for students to demonstrate their effort, we risk exacerbating inequity far more than combating it. Choice is a moral imperative as much as an academic one.

2. Students will experience autonomy, engage in problem solving, and build self-confidence by relying on their skills, notes, and commitments to complete the work independently. For many students, developing confidence includes knowing they can work through academic dilemmas, in part by having the experience of doing so with homework. The turn-and-talks students engage in as part of closure to the lesson are an invaluable time for them to focus on the SEL skills they will need to be successful with homework. One outgrowth of the turn-and-talk can be to establish those pairs of students as "study buddies" who are encouraged to be resources for each other when doing homework. That structure reinforces the SEL skill of advocating for one's needs and resources.

3. Students will use the resources of home and community to explore the curriculum in ways that build their communication skills and socially responsible behavior. The fruits of education should be experienced and expanded outside the school building. My favorite homework assignments engaged my students in their communities. Here are some examples:

- In math classes, for all grade levels, students measured objects or functions in their homes and developed conclusions about the data. (The Greek roots of the word *geometry* literally mean "measuring the Earth"!)
- In language arts classes, students shared their vocabulary words with someone at home and had a dialogue using the words.
- Social studies homework included filling in a checklist of elements in their communities that reflected the SWBATs of the lessons, and surveying adults on the connections they saw between the social studies lesson and their own lives. For students who come from exploited and underresourced families and communities, tying history homework directly to the specific history of their families brings the homework into the SEL realm, as students listen to and grapple with the feelings engendered by the stories of their elders and the ways others have worked for the greater good (Fergus et al., 2014). With so much accumulated content derived from homework, the next day's lesson plan should include a long exploration of what students have delved into in their families and

communities, and robust formative assessment that builds student metacognition.

4. Students will identify their feelings, set personal goals, and work from their strengths as they seek mastery through repetition. Once students have become familiar with certain content, they may need repetitive practice. Chapter 5 considered the possibilities of memorization as part of "messing about," noting that there had to be a compelling story about the facts in order to trigger motivation and prior learning in service of memorization. When assigning repetitive practice for homework, your prompt for the turn-and-talk can focus on the SEL skill of goal setting; for example, for many students, learning how to memorize is a skill they would like to improve.

For some students, the facts to be memorized might relate to their favorite subject, a hobby, or a career. For instance, musicians have to practice basic scales over and over to develop their ear and technique; multiplication tables become second nature through repetition; athletes practice movements to develop the muscle memory needed to perform in the midst of competition; and students of a second language benefit from a lot of drill in conjugating verbs. Homework can be a good time for repetitive drills, leaving more classroom time for higher-order explorations.

But assigning repetitive-drill homework simply to assign homework predicts little achievement. The meaningless repetition can undermine student motivation to put in the time for what really matters. We may also contribute to the likelihood that students won't learn the difference between what is essential and what is mandated; as is, we rarely ask them to consider that crucial difference. Compliance can easily erode commitment, and without the emotional energy of commitment, we breed indifference and mediocrity.

Action Steps

Considering the homework you are assigning, do the following:

- Develop at least four homework options that address the SWBATs from the lesson.
- List the SEL skills that students will most need to exercise in order to be successful with the homework task.
- Craft a prompt for a turn-and-talk appropriate to your students' current functioning and the requirements of this homework.

SEL and the Menu for Closure

Whenever homework is assigned, a brief turn-and-talk as part of closure is always a good idea, if for no other reason than to make sure students know what the homework task is in the midst of all the other mental activity that their brains initiate during a transition. Some teachers will invest in the full version of the homework turn-and-talk as the sole activity of their lesson closure, incorporating all the SEL and executive functioning elements of a homework turn-and-talk. That one activity on its own provides students with a sense of closure before moving on to the next required lesson or responsibility.

But perhaps you aren't assigning homework after every lesson; you have other goals for closure, such as an orderly exit from the room or a chance for everyone to have a brain break. Teachers I have worked with who build a closing ritual into their lesson plans report that their rooms are cleaner and neater, the quality and quantity of homework turned in the next day has increased, their students more often arrive on time to their next responsibility, and the teachers themselves feel calmer and more satisfied.

The menu of closure activities in Figure 7.1 (p. 148) provides opportunities to practice all the SEL skills, once again moving from an implicit and random reinforcement of the skills to an explicit and organized engagement for success. These activities can be done individually (and perhaps shared on an exit ticket), with partners, in small groups, or as a whole class.

Figure 7.2 (p. 150) is a basic exit ticket for students' reflection—allowing them to once again review the lesson and consolidate their understanding and retention. The quiet two minutes that students spend filling out such an exit ticket can be a relaxing ritual and allow you to have brief check-ins with specific students. For the youngest students and those with writing difficulties, the exit ticket prompts can be used for a turn-and-talk or group sharing.

Expressing Gratitude: A Classic SEL Ritual for Closure

Rituals create and bind together communities. Of all the rituals I have implemented for closure, the one I did most frequently focused on gratitude. Almost every time the ritual was complete, the students and I were calm, happy, eager to be with each other again, and, as whole people, more ready for our next responsibility. But even with that great outcome, I didn't use this ritual every day. On some days, there were time constraints and a more pressing agenda. However, each time I skipped this ritual, I felt its absence. As a principal, I also asked the school staff to engage in this ritual at the end of our faculty meetings; the two minutes we spent so engaged contributed a lot to how we operated as a team.

The prompt for the ritual at the end of a lesson is this simple: "Let's have 10 seconds of quiet think time. During the lesson, were there other students who helped you?"

The first few days I introduced this ritual to a class, and until they began to spontaneously contribute to the ritual, I shared a list of ways they may have helped each other, which included the following:

FIGURE 7.1

Prompts for Closure Activities

Skills for Self

Emotional Self-Awareness
 • Let's sit quietly for 30 seconds. All you have to do is breathe.
 • Choose one of our emotion words to describe the following:
    - How confident you feel about the SWBATs of the lesson
    - The effort you made during this lesson

Personal Goal Setting   • What questions and ideas do you still have about the lesson?   • In what ways did you work on your personal SEL goals in this lesson?   • What actions did you take during the lesson, without being told to do so, that helped you learn?   • (For a secondary school class) What do you want to do as you move between this classroom and your next classroom? Make a plan to get to your next class on time.
Identifying Strengths and Supports   • What did you do to help yourself be a good learner in this lesson?   • Before class ends, think about whether there is anything you need so you can be ready for your next responsibility, for going home, or to do homework. This is your time to get your needs met. This is a time to ask for support.
Interpersonal Skills
How Others Feel   • What did you notice about the way anyone else in the class was feeling? Did that distract you, or make you feel like you had an ally, or change you?   • If you reached out to help anyone in the lesson, what made you do so?   • Is there anyone in class you want to check in with or say something to before the next lesson or class, or before the end of the day?
Working with Similarities and Differences   • What did you learn from someone else in class today?   • In what ways did our different ideas make this lesson better for all of us?   • Was there anything we did that helped us hear a lot of different ideas?   • What can we do better to make this a safe learning place for all ideas?

Interpersonal Skills—(*continued*)
Communicating with Others • Choosing from our emotion words, how did it feel for you to speak up in class today? In what ways were you both honest and respectful when you spoke up? • Is there anything that I, as your teacher, could have done differently to help you or the class?
Skills as a Community Member
Having an Impact on Your Community • What did you do during the lesson to help this class be a good place to learn? • Was there anything you refrained from doing in order to help the class be a good place to learn? • When and in what ways did you fix an error, clean up any mess you made, apologize, or correct yourself? How did that go?
Socially Responsible Decision Making • What actions did you take during the lesson, without being told to do so, that helped this class learn? • Is there an action someone else in this class took that you thought helped us all?
Contributing to the Greater Good • What is something you can do in the lesson or class that will make this a better place to learn? • Do you have a suggestion for a new or improved class rule that will help us all work together better?

- Lent you a pencil or an eraser
- Asked a question that helped you understand
- Offered an idea or a solution that helped you understand
- Gave you a compliment or positive feedback
- Asked how you were doing
- Demonstrated how to do the work
- Asked for your support so you got a chance to be helpful
- Made you smile

To help the ritual take root, initially I would always offer my gratitude first, modeling a variety of ways I had seen and heard the class be a community—for example, "I want to thank D. for that amazing question about the color blue; I think it will puzzle me for a long time!" "I want to thank L. and V. for cleaning up the pencil sharpener on their own, without being asked to do so; that's why this class rocks!" "I want to thank B. for noticing that I got a haircut; you made me feel seen." In this case, B. might have been a student who rarely got a shout-out, and my doing so was a strategic move, to give her standing in the class.

To further prompt students to share their gratitude, I would discreetly prompt certain students to be ready for the ritual: "You might want to thank L. at the end of class for his answer to your question" or "Please consider thanking R. at the end of the class for lowering the shade so we could see the video on the screen."

FIGURE 7.2
Sample Exit Ticket for Student Reflection

EXIT TICKET
What I remember most about this lesson:
What I want to know more about:
Something I understand:
What I did well today as a learner:
What I did well today as a classmate:

Action Steps

Based on lessons you referenced throughout this book, do the following:

- Craft up to four turn-and-talk prompts for a closure ritual focused on homework success.
- Choose up to four prompts from the SEL closure chart in Figure 7.1 that can most support your class's SEL development.
- Design a basic exit ticket based on the model in Figure 7.2 that will help your students consolidate more understanding and give you valuable information for the next lesson.
- During the lesson, make note of the many socially responsible behaviors of your students that contribute to their individual SEL development and the class's academic achievement. Use that observation to inspire you to incorporate a short gratitude ritual to close a lesson.

Questions and Answers

I have enough on my mind during a lesson without having to remember that it is time for the closing ritual. I know I will be too distracted to remember this extra responsibility. How can I remind myself?

This is a common concern. We have so much to keep track of in a class filled with students. Luckily, there is a great solution to this dilemma: ask for a student volunteer to alert you when it is time for closure. I am sure you will have little trouble finding a student who will signal you when the time has come to shift into the closing rituals. You can also set a timer to ring—and you will have many student volunteers willing to remind you to set your timer as the lesson begins. You can always include in the Do-Now a request that a student remind you to set your timer for closure.

How do I convince a skeptical supervisor that the closing ritual is an integral part of the lesson and not a touchy-feely activity that reduces the time spent on learning?

Every supervisor is a unique human being, with a unique set of concerns and constraints. You may have to ask a couple of questions to find out the source of concern.

Suggest implementing the closing ritual as a test run for two weeks. Together, choose a couple of before-and-after data points, such as homework completion, retention of academic content, behavior management issues during transitions, condition of the room after transitions, or students referencing progress on goals.

You can also ask the supervisor to observe the ritual and offer feedback. One of the best ways to get a supervisor invested in a test run is to involve that person in the action.

Certainly, suggest the supervisor buy a copy of this book and read the chapter on closure!

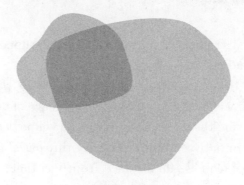

Epilogue

Educator and activist Bill Ayers notes that every class in every school reflects the political and economic system of its setting, from apartheid South Africa to the Soviet Union to the United States. Ayers also notes that in all those disparate settings, teachers have wanted their students to obey them and do the work. He asks us to consider what classrooms would look and sound like if students were taught the skills of actively living in a democracy—that is, the skills to build and participate in a better world (Ayers, 2019).

On the surface, this book has been a journey through every phase of a formal lesson plan. Deeper down, at its heart, I want it to be a source for giving students the experience and skills of participating now in that better world, in your classroom. As noted in the introduction to this book, the term *SEL* is a catchall for a grander aspiration: a practice of creating and sharing our understandings, so that we are collectively wiser, and our hard-earned wisdom is directed to the greater good. We can provide such a learning environment in our classrooms. Administrators can work to create schools that support every classroom in becoming a lively space to walk into every day.

We have the tools right here and right now, richly supported by brain science and studies of child development.

Changing the predominant structures of how we educate all children is going to take a long time. As a principal of a small school, I struggled to find the words, resources, and willpower to carry out many worthy initiatives in that relatively tiny place. Changing our larger system of schools—for instance, from ones that replicate inequity to ones that oppose inequity—will be a long, hard road to travel. There are so many barriers.

Some barriers to changing how our schools function have become undeniably obvious. As I write this book in 2020, during the COVID-19 pandemic and the resurgence of the Black Lives Matter movement, the long and present history of structural racism in the United States is front and center. People of color and poor people die at much higher rates from the virus, Black and brown students are left further behind white students in achievement as schools go virtual, and videos of unarmed Black men and women being shot by police are horrifically repetitive. Whatever your opinion on the issues of racial justice and reparations, the need for continued explicit and direct conversations about racism, how it manifests in our schools, and how to oppose it, is an imperative—and those conversations are happening. Our SEL skills will be critical tools to move those conversations from theory into practice.

The conversations that are not happening, and therefore remain a barrier to the greater good, are conversations about the U.S. economic system. Some call it "free market"; some call it capitalism. In all my years of reading ASCD's catalog of books and articles, I have no memory of seeing the word *capitalism* in print. Yet the economic system profoundly influences every aspect of schooling in the United States, from the proportion of time devoted to SEL skills, to the content of the required curricula, to the role that standardized testing plays in sorting students into winners and losers, to the efficiency of classroom ventilation, to the size of school libraries, to teachers' contracts, to school funding, to access to technology, and to students' hopes to be able to afford a college education—or to have any hopes at all.

Professional basketball player Jaylen Brown (Brown & Kong, 2020) said that growing up poor and Black, he had no idea that the conditions of his community were "not a coincidence," not the fault of his hard-working mother and neighbors. The content of school seemed so disconnected to their needs, so ignorant of their lived reality. He assumed poverty was something to overcome through heroic individual effort, but poverty itself was never the subject of consideration. Not until he was in college did he learn that economic inequality was not inevitable, but a structure integral to the system. It's no surprise that Pope Francis has identified both racism and structural poverty as threatening our collective existence (Gallagher & Benveniste, 2020).

It is said that fish are unaware of the water through which they have swum their entire lives; the economic system in the United States creates the ripples, tides, and tsunamis that determine so much of our lives, including the messages we give to students every day about what is inevitable, what can be understood, and what can be changed. Whether it is a system you revere, tolerate, or criticize, it's time to talk about it. More than 100 years ago, Horace Mann championed public schools as the great equalizer of our democracy, but the lack of economic equality and opportunity outside of schools remains a barrier to that ideal.

Through our lessons and all of our school rituals and procedures, students consistently get the message that they are being prepared to compete for a life in America where falling behind can have disastrous results down the road. That assumption may be true. Parents of kindergarten students are asking for more homework to get their kids ready for more homework later on; those with the economic means are sending their kids to math camps and hiring tutors for the SATs. Most people on the street would probably fail every final exam administered in our high schools, but we push every student to pass every test, lest they face a hard life. As I have noted earlier in this book, rarely do we urge students to learn the curricula because of the contributions they will make to their communities—that most worthy SEL skill. The message is about individual survival.

Teachers are expected to post new SWBATs each day, time on learning is measured by the minute, and arts and music programs are often the first to be slashed as budget cuts squeeze the administration into making choices about what courses will push the school's test scores that extra point higher. This is not a system in which SEL skills naturally flourish—as they should in a setting filled with humans!

No wonder the theories of resilience and grit have found a home in schools; they support the message that kids better toughen up to compete. But to what end, to what worldview, are we relentlessly pushing them so hard? How are our hopes and fears for the adult lives of our students implicitly fueled by the economic forces we all must navigate? Do we have visions for them beyond being compliant employees, beyond fitting in to survive? Maybe in the way that racism is now a prime topic for teacher workshops, professional learning communities, and district initiatives, the word *capitalism* can be spoken, and its impact on all of our efforts in schools can be analyzed. Our adult SEL skills will need to be well honed to begin those conversations.

I hope this book's images and activities for SEL-rich lessons support your vision of a better education—and so a better world for our students. An alternative to grit and resilience is resistance, a pushing against what we know is not right for children, a making of space for them to be their whole selves. I think it is our moral duty to protect our students from being pounded every hour by demands that only some of them are willing and able to take on—not because they aren't tough enough to take it, but because education should mean more than a disempowering compliance that ultimately sustains an inequitable system.

Good lesson plans have an almost mysterious power; they declare that all information can be interesting, that every skill acquired broadens our potential to make a better world, and that all impassioned activity leads to learning. Our best teachers have shown us over and over that life is not a struggle against boredom and compliance; it is a wonder to be apprehended. Every bit of SEL you can integrate into your planning will not only begin to heal the wounds of passivity, racism, and inequity, but also give students an experience today, in your classroom, of that better world.

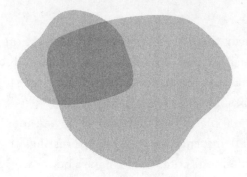

Appendix:
Chapter-by-Chapter
Lesson-Planning Guide

This guide is available for download at www.ascd.org/ASCD/pdf/ books/BensonLessonPlanning.pdf.

Chapter	Teacher Preparation	The Prompts Students Will Hear
1. Making SEL Goals Explicit	Identify the SEL skills that you will prioritize through the year: Identify your professional SEL goal for the year: Identify when to share and model your SEL goal in this lesson:	The prompt students will hear to connect SEL skills to the goals of the lesson: *Students who will benefit from a personalized SEL prompt:* The prompt students will hear to connect SEL skills to the turn-and-talk they will engage in to discuss the goal of the lesson: *Students who will benefit from a personalized SEL prompt:*

Chapter	Teacher Preparation	The Prompts Students Will Hear
2. The Start of the Lesson: Gaining Students' Interest and Motivation	Identify the SEL skills you will emphasize as students settle into the class or lesson:	The prompt students will hear to connect SEL skills to the transition into the room: *Students who will benefit from a personalized SEL prompt:*
	Develop multiple Do-Now options and list them here:	The prompt students will hear to connect SEL skills to the Do-Now: *Students who will benefit from a personalized SEL prompt:*

3. Accessing Prior Learning	Identify the prior learning to reinforce for this lesson:	The prompt students will hear to connect SEL skills to accessing prior learning: *Students who will benefit from a personalized SEL prompt:*
4. Providing and Receiving Direct Instruction	Identify the "need to know" reasons for the content and skills of the direct instruction: Identify your own interest in the content and skills of the direct instruction:	The prompt students will hear to connect SEL skills to direct instruction: *Students who will benefit from a personalized SEL prompt:*

Chapter	Teacher Preparation	The Prompts Students Will Hear
5. Time to Experiment and Discover	Identify the academic skills and content that students can practice during their exploring and experimenting:	The prompt students will hear to connect SEL skills to "See/Think/Wonder" discoveries: *Students who will benefit from a personalized SEL prompt:*
	Identify the SEL skills students will need to use to be successful while sharing and listening to others share their discoveries:	The prompt students will hear to connect SEL skills to making mistakes in explorations: *Students who will benefit from a personalized SEL prompt:*

6. Formative Assessment	Identify the implicit and explicit ways you provide formative assessment: Identify what you are most curious to discover regarding how students are learning during your formative assessment:	The prompt students will hear to connect SEL skills to conferencing during formative assessment: *Students who will benefit from a personalized SEL prompt:* The prompt students will hear to connect SEL skills to risk taking during formative assessment: *Students who will benefit from a personalized SEL prompt:*

Chapter	Teacher Preparation	The Prompts Students Will Hear
7. Closure of the Lesson	Identify the academic, SEL, and executive function goals you want to focus on during lesson closure:	The prompt students will hear to reflect on their use of SEL skills during the lesson:
		Students who will benefit from a personalized SEL prompt:
	Develop closing rituals that reinforce your goals and list them here:	The prompt students will hear to connect SEL skills to pre-viewing homework during lesson closure:
		Students who will benefit from a personalized SEL prompt:

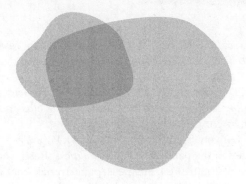

References

Abram, D. (1996). *The spell of the sensual*. Toronto, ON: Random House.

Ayers, W. (2019). *About becoming a teacher*. New York: Teachers College Press.

Benson, J. (2012). 100 repetitions. *Educational Leadership, 70*(2), 76–78.

Benson, J. (2014). *Hanging in: Strategies for teaching the students who challenge us most*. Alexandria, VA: ASCD.

Brooks, J. G., & Brooks, M. G. (2000). *The case for constructivist classrooms: In search of understanding*. Alexandria, VA: ASCD.

Brown, J., & Kong, D. (2020, January 17). Building a bridge for learning. TEDxBeacon Street. Retrieved from https://www.youtube.com/watch?v=nEqkcVU3Oxg

Bryner, J. (2007, July 1). Study reveals why we learn from mistakes. *Live Science*. Retrieved from https://www.livescience.com/7312-study-reveals-learn-mistakes.html

Cox, A. (2007). *No mind left behind*. New York: Penguin.

Duckworth, E. R. (1996). *"The having of wonderful ideas" and other essays on teaching and learning*. New York: Teachers College Press.

Dweck, C. S. (2006). *Mindset: The new psychology of success*. New York: Random House.

Eagleman, D. (2015). *The brain with David Eagleman* (TV series). PBS.

EducationData.org. (n.d.). College dropout rates. Retrieved from https://educationdata.org/college-dropout-rates

Fergus, E., Noguera, P., & Martin, M. (2014). *Schooling for resilience: Improving the life trajectory of Black and Latino boys.* Cambridge, MA: Harvard Education Press.

Frey, N., Fisher, D., & Smith, D. (2019). *All learning is social and emotional: Helping students develop essential skills for the classroom and beyond.* Alexandria, VA: ASCD.

Gallagher, D., & Benveniste, A. (2020, October 4). Pope Francis says capitalism has failed in the pandemic. *CNN Business.* Retrieved from https://www.cnn.com/2020/10/04/business/pope-francis-market-capitalism

Hammond, Z. (2015). *Culturally responsive teaching and the brain: Promoting authentic engagement and rigor among culturally and linguistically diverse students.* Thousand Oaks, CA: Corwin.

Hattie, J. (2009). *Visible learning: A synthesis of meta-analyses relating to achievement.* London: Routledge.

Hawkins, D. (1965). Messing about in science. *Science and Children, 2*(5). Retrieved from https://www.colorado.edu/ftep/sites/default/files/attached-files/ftep_memo_to_faculty_42.pdf

Hoerr, T. R. (2017). *The formative five: Fostering grit, empathy, and other success skills every student needs.* Alexandria, VA: ASCD.

Immordino-Yang, M. H. (2016). *Emotions, learning, and the brain: Exploring the educational implications of affective neuroscience.* New York: W. W. Norton.

Jacobson, M. D. (2013, September). Afraid of looking dumb. *Educational Leadership, 71*(1), 40–43.

Jensen, E. (2009). *Teaching with poverty in mind: What being poor does to kids' brains and what schools can do about it.* Alexandria, VA: ASCD.

Love, B. L. (2019, February 12). "Grit is in our DNA": Why teaching grit is inherently anti-Black. *Education Week.* Retrieved from https://www.edweek.org/ew/articles/2019/02/13/grit-is-in-our-dna-why-teaching.html

McTighe, J., & Willis, J. (2019). *Upgrade your teaching: Understanding by Design meets neuroscience.* Alexandria, VA: ASCD.

Medina, J. (2009). *Brain rules: 12 principles for surviving and thriving at work, home, and school.* Seattle, WA: Pear Press.

Milner, H. R., IV. (2017, November). Confronting inequity/reimagining the null curriculum. *Educational Leadership, 75*(3), 88–89. Retrieved from http://www.ascd.org/publications/educational-leadership/nov17/vol75/num03/Reimagining-the-Null-Curriculum.aspx

O'Connell, S. (2017, September 14). What really happened when Harrison Ford gave George Lucas crap on set. *Cinema Blend.* Retrieved from https://www.cinemablend.com/news/1702860/what-really-happened-when-harrison-ford-gave-george-lucas-crap-on-set

Poliner, R. A., & Benson, J. (2017). *Teaching the whole teen: Everyday practices that promote success and resilience in school and life.* Thousand Oaks, CA: Corwin.

Quaglia, R. J., & Corso, M. J. (2014). *Student voice: The instrument of change.* Thousand Oaks, CA: Corwin.

Ritchie, S. (2015). *Intelligence: All that matters.* London: John Murray Press.

Rothstein, D., & Santana, L. (2011). *Make just one change: Teach students to ask their own questions.* Cambridge, MA: Harvard Education Press.

Souers, K., with Hall, P. (2016). *Fostering resilient learners: Strategies for creating a trauma-sensitive classroom.* Alexandria, VA: ASCD.

Tatum, A. W. (2005). *Teaching reading to Black adolescent males: Closing the achievement gap.* Portland, ME: Stenhouse.

Warrington, M. A. (1997). How children think about division with fractions. *Mathematics Teaching in the Middle School, 2*(6), 390–394.

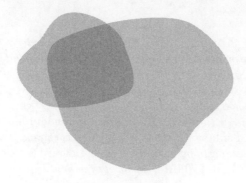

Index

Page references followed by an italicized *f* indicate information contained in figures.

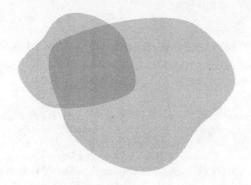

About the Author

Jeffrey Benson has more than 40 years of experience as a teacher, mentor, and school administrator, with a focus on supporting schools that can work for all students. He has worked on initiatives involving school reform, conflict resolution, learning theory, trauma and addiction, school advisory programs, math education, staff development, leadership training, and curriculum development. He is a member of the ASCD Faculty, is frequently published in education journals, and speaks at conferences on such topics as working with challenging students, developing safe and welcoming school cultures, and implementing best practices for inclusion. His books include *Hanging In: Strategies for Working with the Students Who Challenge Us Most, 10 Steps for Managing Change in Schools,* and *Teaching the Whole Teen: Everyday Practices That Promote Success and Resilience in School and Life.* His website is JeffreyBenson.org.

Related ASCD Resources: SEL and Lesson Planning

At the time of publication, the following resources were available (ASCD stock numbers appear in parentheses).

Print Products

All Learning Is Social and Emotional: Helping Students Develop Essential Skills for the Classroom and Beyond by Nancy Frey, Douglas Fisher, and Dominique Smith (#119033)

The Equity & Social Justice Education 50: Critical Questions for Improving Opportunities and Outcomes for Black Students by Baruti K. Kafele (#121060)

Hanging In: Strategies for Teaching the Students Who Challenge Us Most by Jeffrey Benson (#114013)

The i5 Approach: Lesson Planning That Teaches Thinking and Fosters Innovation by Jane E. Pollock with Susan Hensley (#117030)

Learning in the Making: How to Plan, Execute, and Assess Powerful Makerspace Lessons by Jackie Gerstein (#119025)

Level Up Your Classroom: The Quest to Gamify Your Lessons and Engage Your Students by Jonathan Cassie (#116007)

The Power of Place: Authentic Learning Through Place-Based Education by Tom Vander Ark, Emily Liebtag, and Nate McClennen (#120017)

The Purposeful Classroom: How to Structure Lessons with Learning Goals in Mind by Douglas Fisher and Nancy Frey (#112007)

Relationship, Responsibility, and Regulation: Trauma-Invested Practices for Fostering Resilient Learners by Kristin Van Marter Souers with Pete Hall (#119027)

The Relevant Classroom: 6 Steps to Foster Real-World Learning by Eric Hardie (#120003)

Student Learning Communities: A Springboard for Academic and Social-Emotional Development by Douglas Fisher, Nancy Frey, and John Almarode (#121030)

Taking Social-Emotional Learning Schoolwide: The Formative Five Success Skills for Students and Staff by Thomas R. Hoerr (#120014)

Teaching for Deeper Learning: Tools to Engage Students in Meaning Making by Jay McTighe and Harvey F. Silver (#120022)

For up-to-date information about ASCD resources, go to **www.ascd.org**. You can search the complete archives of *Educational Leadership* at **www.ascd.org/el**.

Video

All Learning Is Social and Emotional: The Hidden Curriculum by Nancy E. Frey, Douglas B. Fisher, and Dominique Smith (#620046VS)

PD Online

Fostering Resilient Learners (#PD11OC001S)

ASCD myTeachSource®

Download resources from a professional learning platform with hundreds of research-based best practices and tools for your classroom at http://myteachsource.ascd.org/.

For more information, send an e-mail to member@ascd.org; call 1-800-933-2723 or 703-578-9600; send a fax to 703-575-5400; or write to Information Services, ASCD, 1703 N. Beauregard St., Alexandria, VA 22311-1714 USA.